IN THE NAME OF GOD

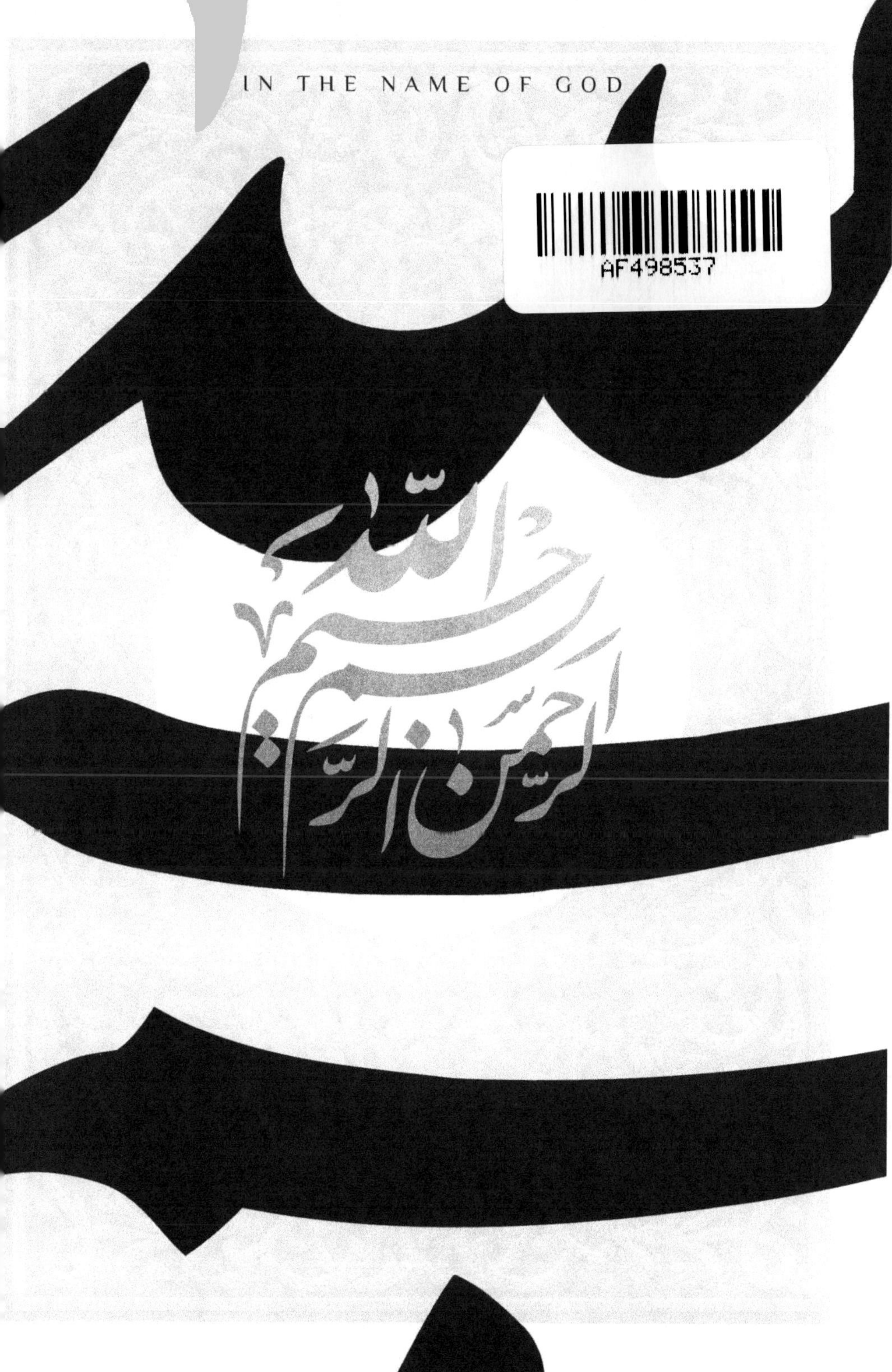
IN THE NAME OF GOD

HIGH ABOVE THE HEAVENS

HIGH ABOVE THE HEAVENS

HIGH ABOVE THE HEAVENS

Title: High Above the Heavens
Authored by: Mostafa Mollababazadeh, Amir Rastin
Commissioned by: The Management of Foreign Pilgrims of the A.Q.R., Islamic Relations Office
Published by: Za'er Razavi
Edited by: Tina Marie Huskey
Proofread by: Mahsa Raeisi Sattari
Graphic Artist: Sayyed Ali Assaran
Circulation: 1000 copies
Printed by: The Astan Qods Razavi Printing and Publishing Institute

عنوان: بر فراز آسمان

نویسنده: مصطفی ملابابازاده، امیر راستین
به سفارش: مدیریت زائرین غیر ایرانی آستان قدس رضوی، اداره ارتباطات اسلامی
ویراستار: تینا مری هاسکی
نمونه‌خوان: مهسا رئیسی ستاری
طراح: سید علی عصاران
ناشر: زائر رضوی
چاپ: موسسه چاپ و انتشارات آستان قدس رضوی
چاپ اول: ۱۴۴۲ ق. / ۲۰۲۰ م.
تیراژ: ۱۰۰۰ نسخه

سرشناسه: ملاباباراده، مصطفی، 1360 - مولف
Mollababazadeh, Mostafa

عنوان و نام پدیدآور:
High Above the Heavens [Book] / Authored by: Mustafa Mollababazadeh,
Amir Rastin; Edited by: Tina Marie Huskey; Commissioned by: The Management
of Foreign Pilgrims of the A.Q.R., Islamic Relations Office;
Published by the Islamic Propagation Department of the A.Q.R.

مشخصات نشر: مشهد، زائر رضوی، 1399=2020 م.
مشخصات ظاهری: 88 ص 5/14 5/21 س.م.
شابک: 9-15-6852-622-978
وضعیت فهرست نویس: فیپا
یادداشت: انگلیسی
یادداشت: عنوان به فارسی: برفراز آسمان
موضوع: خاندان نبوت
موضوع: Muhammad, the Prophet (P.B.U.H.), d. 632-Family
موضوع: زیارت و زائران مسلمان
موضوع: Pilgrimage and Muslim pilgrims
موضوع: زیارتگاه های اسلامی
موضوع: Islamic shrines
شناسه افزوده: راستین امیر، 1367، مولف
شناسه افزوده: Rastin, Amir
شناسه افزوده: هاسکی، تینا ماری، ویراستار
شناسه افزوده: Huskey, Tina Marie
شناسه افزوده: رئیسی، مهسا، نمونه خوان
شناسه افزوده: Raeisi, Mahsa
شناسه افزوده: مدیریت زائرین غیر ایرانی استان قدس رضوی
شناسه افزوده: The Management of Foreign Pilgrims
شناسه افزوده: معاونت تبلیغات اسلامی آستان قدس رضوی
شناسه افزوده: The Islamic Propagation Department
رده بندی کنگره: BP262/ه 8 م ـ 1398
رده بندی دیویی: 76/297
شماره کتابشناسی ملی: 6846568

Table of Contents

Introduction

Higher than the Heavens

Imam al-Kāẓim (P.B.U.H.) stated, "One who visits the tomb of my son, ʿAlī b. Mūsā al-Riḍā (P.B.U.H.), their reward unto God is equal to seventy approved Hajj... even more than that! Their reward is equal to seventy thousand approved Hajj!... and it is perhaps not a surprise that many people go to Hajj, but their Hajj isn't approved by God, yet one who goes to visit my son, ʿAlī (P.B.U.H.), and gets to sleep for a night in his holy shrine is similar to one who has gone up to the Divine Throne (*the ʿArsh*) and visited Almighty God there, and when the Day of Judgment arrives, four people from the former generations and four people from the later ones will be (seated) on the Divine *ʿArsh*. Here are the four people of the past: Noah, Abraham, Moses, and Jesus Christ (P.B.U.T.); and the four people of the later times are: the holy Prophet Muḥammad, Imam ʿAlī, Imam al-Ḥasan, and Imam al-Ḥussain (P.B.U.T.), ... Then the visitors of the Infallible Imams' (P.B.U.T.) holy shrines will be seated along with us, *Ahl al-Bayt* (P.B.U.T.), on the Divine *'Arsh*! Be aware of the fact that the highest positions and the best rewards belong to the visitors of the tomb of my son, 'Alī (P.B.U.H.).[1]

Regarding the matter of visiting *Ahl al-Bayt* (P.B.U.T.)[2], there is a practical part which is the concept of light and recognizing *Ahl al-Bayt* (P.B.U.T.) as light. According to the divine invitation by *Ahl al-Bayt* (P.B.U.T.), we have to look for these dignitaries through recognizing them as light. But why should we follow this matter? What is the product of such a conception?

In this world, man has been put into darkness and it is necessary for him to move on a specific path through his deeds so that he can find and enter into the light and see *Ahl al-Bayt* (P.B.U.T.) and their lights. One of the reasons behind the necessity of entering into the light is the fact that we can see through that light[3] and according to the traditions, this light is the light of *Ahl al-Bayt* (P.B.U.T.) which is shining in all parts of the skies and the earth.[4]

---

1. Kulaynī, M. (1407 A.H.), *Al-Kāfī*, Tehran: Dār al-Kutub al-Islāmīya, vol.4, p. 585.
2. '*Ahl al-Bayt*' is a title used for the infallible progeny of the Holy Prophet (peace be upon him and his household) in the holy Qur'an, "Indeed Allah desires to repel all impurity from you, O People of the Household, and purify you with a thorough purification." (33: 33)
3. The holy Prophet (P.B.U.H. & H.H.) said, "Stay away from the believer›s perspicacity and their good observation for achieving something, because a believer looks at everything through the light of Almighty God." (*Al-Kāfī*, vol. 1, p. 218)
4. Daylamī, H. (1412 A.H.), *Irshād al-Qulūb*, Qom: al-Sharīf al-Raḍī, vol2. p. 403.

With respect to these concepts, some matters have a conceptual dimension, but what is that practical dimension? Will our knowledge and viewpoints lead us to consider some majesty and sanctity toward *Ahl al-Bayt* (P.B.U.T.) or not? Will it make us humble toward them? If yes, thus, we have to know that we are starting to understand them through the concept of light, we are beginning to perceive them *high* and perceive ourselves *low* and humble.

This concept is clear in *Āyat al-Kursī* (2: 255-257) that is highly emphasized to be read in different situations. According to the third verse of it, we can see that there is darkness on world's surface and in such an atmosphere one is on the verge of downfall, but Allah, as the Protector of the believers, brings them out of darkness into light. [1]

It's obvious that light comes from above and the sky, and not from below and the earth. Also with respect to the matter of sustenance, Almighty God says,

$$وَ فِي السَّماءِ رِزْقُكُمْ وَ ما تُوعَدُونَ$$

And in the sky is your provision and what you are promised.
(51: 22)

Allah has decided to send the sustenance and other

---

1. Allah is the *walī* of the faithful: He brings them out of darkness into light. As for the faithless, their *awlīyā* are the fake deities, who drive them out of light into darkness. They shall be the inmates of the Fire, and they will remain in it [forever].

affairs from the heavens down to the earth, these movements are made from up to down; therefore, when man wants to request for sustenance, they raise their hands toward the heavens and look upward and start to pray. With respect to this verse, the Chief of the Faithful (P.B.U.H.) answered this question that why we raise our hands toward the heavens when we pray.[1]

This sustenance is directed from obove, and if one wants to request for it, they must look upwards. Therefore, the feeling of height is the product of recognizing *Ahl al-Bayt* (P.B.U.T.) as the light.

Now we want to survey this concept with regard to the matter of *Zīyārah* (visiting the holy shrines of *Ahl al-Bayt* (P.B.U.T.)) and, while discussing the matter, answer this important question that what our intellectual atmosphere and definition of the concept of *Zīyārah* is.

For instance, when we say: let's go to Mashhad for visiting Imam al-Riḍā (P.B.U.H.), by the word *visit* we imply that we are here and Imam al-Riḍā (P.B.U.H.)–for example–is 500 kilometers ahead, we are going to visit him. However, this matter is different from the concept of *height.* In the pure culture of the Shia–for example–when someone is asked, "Where do you want to go?" they say, "I want to go to the presence of the world's Imam." It means they

---

1. Ibn Shu'bi, Ḥ. (1404 A.H.), *Tuḥaf al-'Uqūl*, Qom: Jami'i Modarresīn, p. 118.

use a word which creates a feeling of height toward Imam in themselves and in the second person; and it creates a feeling of holiness in both sides.

Holiness means that the Imams are so high and before them, I am so lowly; they are so high-ranking and commanding and I am so low-ranking and modest; and one of the best concepts of holiness is the fact that one should look at *Ahl al-Bayt* (P.B.U.T.) in a way that the feeling of height distinction and a distinction between the essence of visitor and *Ahl al-Bayt* (P.B.U.T.) can be perceived. One should say the word of visit in a way that the feeling of height would be evoked in themselves and their addressee and they have to consider an atmosphere of *presence* and even more than that, a particular presence and floating in the light of the Imams, that is, they are supposed to see themselves as a dandelion in the atmosphere of sunlight.

Or one can say, "I want to go to the presence of the world's king." What is of importance in a visit is that the atmosphere of presence should be noticeable. We should accustom ourselves to this matter and foster such a culture at the time of going to Mashhad or to other holy shrines, and should say, "We are going to the presence of world's king" rather than saying, "We are going to Imam al-Riḍā (P.B.U.H.)." It's the holy Qur'an that frequently highlights that,

لِلَّهِ مُلْكُ السَّماواتِ وَالْأَرْضِ

To Allah belongs the kingdom of the heavens and the earth.[1]

Due to the fact that the infallible Imams (P.B.U.T.) are the successors of God, they are the purpose of these verses that the kingdom of heavens and the earth belongs to them by God's permission.

A Shiite should even be attentive to the terms and the words they use for Imams and for the *Zīyārah*. We have to use the terms and words which indicate the concept of *height* and, accordingly, influence our deeds and behavior. We have to measure ourselves according to such matters and see which one of us regards Imams as the kings of the heavens and the earth. Moreover, one should say in their *Zīyārah*, "I have come to the presence of the owner of the Divine *'Arsh*." It means the people who have stood in this holy place must feel a need for raising their heads toward the heavens, and due to the majesty of the presence, they must put down their heads.

There is an exalted concept within the word of *Zīyārah* and when the concept of presence and the feeling of height are understood from it, its value will be revealed.

---

1. For instance, see *the holy Qur'an*, 5: 17, 18, 40, 120.

The Importance of Visiting *Ahl al-Bayt* (P.B.U.T.)

Visiting the holy shrines of *Ahl al-Bayt* (P.B.U.T.) has a lot of advantages and benefits for the personal, social, and spritual life, therefore, it has strongly been emphasized in the traditions of these infallible dignitaries (P.B.U.T.), and their practice and the practice of their Shiites such as the great scholars attest to the importance of this fact.

According to the belief of Shiite, visiting *Ahl al-Bayt* (P.B.U.T.) is a way to move toward perfection. This is why the Shiite scholars and dignitaries have frequently tried to clarify this matter and compiled many valuable books and articles with respect to it, but the extensiveness and the greatness of this matter–which has caused the enemies and the opponents of *Ahl al-Bayt* (P.B.U.T.) to destroy their holy shrines and humiliate them and also led them to impute *Shirk* (polytheism) to the pilgrims–necessitates paying more attention to the matter of visiting *Ahl al-Bayt* (P.B.U.T.) and its advantages, especially visiting the holy shrine of our Protector, Imam ʿAlī Ibn Musa al-Riḍā (P.B.U.H.).

It has been narrated that once Diʿbil b. ʿAlī al-Khuzaʿī, who was a dutiful Shiite poet came to Imam al-Riḍā (P.B.U.H.) at Marv and recited his noble poem known as "ballad of *Tāʾiyya*"[1] in the presence of Imam (P.B.U.H.). When Diʿbil,

---

1. The full text of this valuable ballade has been brought in different resources such as: Irbilī, ʿA. (1381 A.H.), *Kashf al-Qummah*, Tabriz: Banīhāshimī, vol.2, pp. 318-327.

after mentioning shiny places and sacred tombs of the oppressed children of Lady Fāṭima (P.B.U.H.), mentioned the sacred body buried in Baghdad (that is Imam al-Kāẓim (P.B.U.H.)), in order to emphasize and complete his lengthy and meaningful ballade, Imam al-Riḍā (P.B.U.H.) told him about a saddening and heart rending tomb which will be in the land of Ṭūs and adds these two lines to his ballade,

"And a grave is in Ṭūs; what a sorrowful tragedy it is!

Through sighs, it would keep blazing [a profound grief] in the heart

Until the Resurrection, when Allah sends the Riser

[Imam al-Mahdī (May God hasten his advent)]

Who relieves us from the distresses and griefs."

Di'bil asked the Imam (P.B.U.H.), "Whose tomb is this which is in Ṭus?" Imam al-Riḍā (P.B.U.H.) answered, "This is my own tomb; after not many days and nights, my Shi-ites and pilgrims will travel to it. One who visits me in my loneliness at Ṭus, in the Day of Judgment, they will be along with me in my position and their sin will be forgiven." Then the Imam (P.B.U.H.) stood up and bestowed a gift to Di'bil in order to admire him for his poem.[1]

Also according to some traditions, when a friend of *Ahl al-Bayt* (P.B.U.T.) intends to go to visit the holy shrine of Imam al-Ḥussain (P.B.U.H.), seventy hundred angels are

---

1. Ibid., p. 327.

told to go to the hometown of that person to welcome him. Therefore, the angels accompany him until he arrives to the holy shrine. When his *Zīyārah* is finished, a summoner calls that, "Now you are clean of all your sins." When the pilgrim intends to return to his city, those angels are summoned to accompany him until he arrives to his hometown. When they arrive to his home, they pray for him, and they will visit him every day until his death. They will also visit the holy shrine of Imam al-Ḥussain (P.B.U.H.) every day on behalf of him and the rewards of it belongs to that person."[1]

You may ask how such unbelievable bounties and blessings are possible! The answer is not that much difficult: God, the Almighty, has stated,

فَاذْكُرُونِی اَذْكُرْکُم

Remember Me ,and I will remember you. (2: 152)

During the occasion of making visit, if the Imam who is being visited is placed in the mind and heart of the pilgrim, then the pilgrim will also be in the mind and heart of the Imam. When one says Salam to the holy Prophet and the infallible Imams (P.B.U.T.), they will certainly answer and pay attention. In *Idhn al-Dukhūl* (a supplication recited upon entering the shrines of the Infallibles (P.B.U.T.), as

---

1. See: Ibn Qūlawayh, J. (1356 A.H. (solar)), *Kāmil al-Zīyārāt*, Najaf: Dār al-Murtaḍavīyya, p. 190.

a request for permission), there is such an expression addressing God,

"And I know that–indeed–the holy Prophet and his successors (P.B.U.T.) are alive, and near You they are provided for, and they see my position and hear my words and answer my Salam."[1]

If our Salam and greeting is conveyed to the holy Prophet and *Ahl al-Bayt* (P.B.U.T.), don't they give a benediction and favor to us? Yes! Here the affection is not one-sided. *Ahl al-Bayt* (P.B.U.T.) are alive and existent and care about the pilgrim of their shrine. Because they are the Imams of mercy and it is impossible that they return their visitors empty handed. When a pilgrim enters the holy shrine of Imam al-Riḍā (P.B.U.H.), for example, he pours the rain of graces on him and helps him to move on the way of growth toward the top of the divine *'Arsh.*

Thus, we shouldn't look at the visit of Imam al-Riḍā (P.B.U.H.) and other *Ahl al-Bayt* (P.B.U.T.) through a materialistic viewpoint and regard the span of their shrine as a tomb or ultimately a *Ḍarīḥ* (brassy lattice windows surrounding the holy tomb). According to many traditions, like that of Imam al-Kāẓim (P.B.U.H.) which was mentioned at the beginning, a pilgrimage has the potential to take the pilgrim toward the summit of the Divine *'Arsh!* Also

---

1. Kaf'amī, I. (1405 A.H.), *al-Miṣbāḥ*, Qom: Dār Al-Raḍī, p. 473.

Shaykh Kulaynī has narrated from Imam al-Riḍā (P.B.U.H.) saying, "One who visits Imam al-Ḥussain (P.B.U.H.) around the river of Furat is like the one who has visited Allah on top of the 'Arsh."[1]

Of course, the scale of benefiting from these divine graces depends on the recognition one has about them; with respect to this matter, Imam al-Ṣādiq (P.B.U.H.) says, "Surely, one who visits the tomb of Ḥussain Ibn 'Alī (P.B.U.T.) along with having the recognition of his right, Almighty God writes that they are among the 'Illīyyūn.[2]"[3] It means that Almighty God will bestow this grace on them so that they can be included among the celestial and heavenly people.

Therefore, a pilgrim needs to achieve the recognition of *Ahl al-Bayt* (P.B.U.T.) and perceive the true meaning of visiting their holy shrines, and have a correct viewpoint toward these dignitaries and their holy shrines so that they can benefit from their blessed visit as *Ahl al-Bayt* (P.B.U.T.) expect them to do.

Let's spiritually swim in the light of *Ahl al–Bayt* (P.B.U.T.) when we go in their shiny holy shrines.

---

1. *Kāmil al-Zīyārāt*, p. 147.
2. To know more about *'Illīyyūn*, refer to the holy Qur'an (83: 18-19).
3. *Kāmil al-Zīyārāt*, p. 147.

Viewpoints About the Holy Shrines of *Ahl al-Bayt* (P.B.U.T.)

In making pilgrimage to the shrine of Imam al-Riḍā (P.B.U.H.) and other *Ahl al-Bayt* (P.B.U.T.) there are various perspectives for different kinds of pilgrims. Some of these perspectives are more valuable and practical than others. According to the narratives said about the extent of advantages that pilgrims can take from the pilgrimage to *Ahl al-Bayt*'s (P.B.U.T.) shrines and the degree of their knowledge, it can be said that the extent of individuals' benefit gained by the pilgrimage depends on their perception and knowledge; in other words, there is a difference between a pilgrim who thinks that the person visited was an Imam in a particular time, and now is buried in this place, in comparison with the one who believes that the Imam is an entrance to God, and God has created the whole universe and human being due to the existence of his entity; he is entitled to all of God's Excellent Names[1] and he is the treasurer of God's knowledge and the mediator for the graces, blessings and mercies of Him in all times and places.[2]

1. Explaining the verse, "To Allah belong the Best Names, so supplicate Him by them" (7: 180), Imam Ṣādiq (a) said, "Swear to God that we, the *Ahl al-Bayt*, are the "Best Names" and God will not accept any deeds from His servants except with having recognition towards us." (*Al-Kāfī*, vol.1, p. 143.).
2. We read in the *Zīyārat of Imam Ḥussain* (P.B.U.H.), "Doubtlessly, I have arrived to certainty that God, whose praise is majestic, removes distresses and troubles through you and takes away the misadventures and mishaps by way of

One shouldn't deprive himself of the graces and blessings of God by having a weak perception toward *Ahl al-Bayt* (P.B.U.T.) which creates a veil between the light of Imam and that person. A person should go on a pilgrimage with the knowledge that would be entitled to the Imam. There are some attitudes based on verses and narratives about the shrines of *Ahl al-Bayt* (P.B.U.T.) that one can take.

1. Considering the Shrines as the *Bayt* (House)

Regarding the perspective of *Bayt*, we can hint at *Sūra* Nūr, verse number 35 to 38.[1]

We should focus on the verse number 36,

> In *houses* Allah has allowed to be raised and wherein His Name is
>
> celebrated; He is glorified therein, morning and evening.

you; and He eliminates the afflictions and pains by you and He initiates (His creation) by means of you and He descends the abundant and far-spread rain and His mercy on account of you. He has stabilized the earth so that it doesn't immerse its habitants because of you, and He has prevented the mountains to move and made them stable by means of you." (Ṭūsī, M. (1407 A.H.), *Tahdhīb Al-Aḥkām*, Tehran: Dār al-Kutub al-Islāmīya, vol. 6, p. 60.)

1. Allah is the Light of the heavens and the earth. The parable of His Light is a niche wherein is a lamp—the lamp is in a glass, the glass as it were a glittering star—lit from a blessed olive tree, neither eastern nor western, whose oil almost lights up, though fire should not touch it. Light upon light. Allah guides to His Light whomever He wishes. Allah draws parables for mankind, and Allah has knowledge of all things. (35) In *houses* Allah has allowed to be raised and wherein His Name is celebrated; He is glorified therein, morning and evening, (36) [by] men whom neither trade nor bargaining distracts from the remembrance of Allah and the maintenance of prayer and the giving of zakat. They are fearful of a day wherein the hearts and the sights will be transformed, (37) so that Allah may reward them by the best of what they have done, and enhance them out of His grace, and Allah provides for whomever He wishes without any reckoning. (38)

God has put some prominent qualities in these *houses* that allow humans to exalt Almighty God; it means that out of these places exaltation isn't allowed or isn't as allowable as inside them. According to this verse, if one exalts God in such places, the result is what comes in the next verse:

So it can be concluded that the exaltation of God outside these houses isn't that worthy, and exalting God in these houses will lead to the verse 37 and then to the verse 38 that,

It means that Allah grants them their needs and even the things that they can't imagine. It's for the people who have found these houses, have come into these houses and have kept the remembrance of God there.

If we look at these four verses concurrently, they will show us that there is a light in the realm of the heavens and the earth. This light is belonging to God, "Allah is the light of the heavens and the earth", and guiding is its characteristic, "Allah guides to His light whom He wills". This light is not the light of guidance, but its effect is in

the shape of guidance. The example of this light is like a lamp that radiates in all directions and imparts to all human beings. However, it isn't possible to receive benefits from this light everywhere or in every part of the heavens and the earth! But there are only some special places where one can be benefited.

Here the most important question is raised: "What houses are these houses?"

Perhaps, one would say that these houses are 'mosques' and if one only goes into a mosque and prays to God, he would benefit from the meanings of these verses. But it is not the case. Because on the one hand, it has been said in the narratives related to this verse that this verse, word by word, is about the progeny of the holy Prophet (P.B.U.T.).[1] On the other hand, there are a lot of mosques where you can't find even a single sign of *Ahl al-Bayt* (P.B.U.T.), and there there is no regard for *Ahl al-Bayt* (P.B.U.T.) by the people in those mosques and even some of them have been founded to antagonize the progeny of the holy Prophet (P.B.U.T.).

So the best examples of these houses are the luminous entities of *Ahl al-Bayt* (P.B.U.T.).[2]

---

1. *Al-Kāfī*, vol. 1, p. 195.
2. Baḥrānī, H. (1374 A.H. (solar)), *Al-Burhān fī Tafsīr al-Qur'an*, Qom: Be'that, vol. 4, pp. 72-73; According to traditions, the same is true about the meaning of 'house' in the verse 189 of *Sūra* al-Baqarah: Aṣbagh b. Nubāta says, "I was sitting beside

Once Qatāda (a great Sunni interpreter) came to Imam al-Bāqir (P.B.U.H.) to ask some questions. After hearing the Imam's (P.B.U.H.) words, he pondered for a while and then said, "O' Master! I Swear to God that I have sat beside the greatest scholars and I have been in the presence of Ibn 'Abbās, but my heart never shook as it was shaken by your words. The Imam (P.B.U.H.) said, "Do you know where you are? You are in the presence of a family whom God has allowed them to pray to Him and exalt His Name and they are remembering God every day and night. Neither trade nor bargaining distracts them from the remembrance of Allah and the maintenance of prayer and giving *Zakat*. You are standing in such place and we are that family." Qatāda said, "O' Master! May I be sacrificed for you! Undoubtedly you are right. The houses (that God has mentioned in *Sūra Nūr*) are not the clay and stony houses but you are those houses."[1]

Imam 'Alī (P.B.U.H.) when Ibn al-Kawā came and said, "O' Commander of the Faithful (P.B.U.H.)! Who are the purpose of the houses in the words of Almighty God where he says, "And it is not righteousness to enter houses from the back, but righteousness is [in] one who fears Allah and enters houses from their doors." Commander of the Faithful (P.B.U.H.) said, "We are those houses that Allah has ordered to enter from their doors, we are the doors of Allah and we are the houses that all things are given through them, so whoever obeys us and admits out guardianship, doubtlessly he has entered into the houses through their doors, and whoever opposes us and prefers another person instead of us, he has strayed and has entered in these houses from the back." (Ṭabrisī, A. (1403 A.H.), *Al-Iḥtijāj 'Alā Ahl Al-Lijāj*, Mashhad: Al-Murtaḍā pub., vol. 1, p.227.)

1. *Al-Kāfī*, vol. 6, p. 256.

Ahl al-Bayt (P.B.U.T.), who are the biggest divine favors bestowed upon the creatures, aren't limited to any time or any place and the light of *Imamate* (leadership) can guide the people in all periods. This light was glowing on all creatures and living beings of the supernatural and natural world and also it is glowing now. But to utilize this favor, people should enter in its realm; they should come in these houses and then they begin to pray to God, the Almighty, and obey Him. These honorable dignitaries lived for a period of time in this world with physical bodies, but now what can we do when we don't have access to their luminous bodies?

Man isn't limited spiritually, hereupon, he can constantly think about *Ahl al-Bayt* (P.B.U.T.) and enter in these houses and reside there spiritually. Man can emotionally and internally accompany with *Ahl al-Bayt* (P.B.U.T.) forever and swim in their heavenly sea of light, because the world is in the presence of God and *Ahl al-Bayt* (P.B.U.T.) as His successors.

However, to enjoy a more palpable sense of relationship with these Divine lights after their demise, we can enter their holy shrines. Because after the sacred entities of *Ahl al-Bayt* (P.B.U.T.), their holy shrines[1] hold the second rank in the concept of 'house'. They themselves set a high value on these holy shrines and used to put stress on the

---

1. Explaining the verse 38 of *Sūra Nūr*, Imam Ṣādiq (P.B.U.H.) said, "It means the houses of the holy Prophet (P.B.U.H. & H.H.)." (*Al-Kāfī*, vol. 8, p. 331.)

visit to these places. Therefore, entering the holy shrines of these dignitaries in company with having faith in their leadership and guardianship is another interpretation of the houses in *Sūra Nūr.*

We as Shiites believe that *Ahl al-Bayt* (P.B.U.T.) are alive and their holy shrines aren't actually their tomb and burial place; the viewpoint of tomb is somehow superficial. The interior fact is that these martyr dignitaries are alive and their shrines are their houses. As Almighty God says in the holy Qur'an,

وَلَا تَحْسَبَنَّ الَّذِينَ قُتِلُوا فِي سَبِيلِ اللَّهِ أَمْوَاتًا بَلْ أَحْيَاءٌ عِنْدَ رَبِّهِمْ يُرْزَقُونَ

Do not suppose those who were slain in the way of Allah to be dead;
no ,they are living and provided for near their Lord (3:169).

Therefore, according to thousands of reasons, *Ahl al-Bayt* (P.B.U.T.) were always alive and are alive forever and ever and their martyrdom is the extra-proved reason about their existence and life. That is why we don't see them into the grave when we visit these dignitaries, but we look at them in a way that the landlord is alive and welcomes and receives his guests. If man looks to the matter from this perspective, when they go to the house of the Imams (P.B.U.T.), their behavior and thoughts toward them will be different from the people who have another perspective and such a person can take more advantage of these dignitaries' light.

There are fourteen houses man can choose any of which he likes and goes toward it, comes in and resides in it. That's what God wants mankind to do. He wants them to go into these houses and then pray to Him. This means that they should first accept the progeny of the holy Prophet (P.B.U.T. & H.H) and by going under their light of Imamate, guardianship and guidance, pray to Almighty God.

In the presence of God, it isn't that much important whether one establishes the prayer or not, but the point is that *'where'* he establishes the prayer. Was it through the light of Imamate, guardianship and guidance of *Ahl al-Bayt* (P.B.U.T.) or not?

It has been quoted from Muyassir who said, "I came to Imam al-Ṣādiq (P.B.U.H.) and said, "May I be sacrificed for you! I have a neighbor who awakes me by his voice; he recites the holy Qur'an and repeats the verses, cries, wails and prays a lot. I've asked others about his deeds, they say that he keeps himself away from every unlawful thing." The Imam (P.B.U.H.) said, "O' Muyassir! Does he believe in Imamate and guardianship as you believe?" I said, "God knows better." Then Muyassir says, "The next year I went to Hajj and asked about his belief and realized that he doesn't believe in the guardianship of *Ahl al-Bayt* (P.B.U.H.). Again I came to Imam al-Ṣādiq (P.B.U.H.) and talked about that man. The Imam (P.B.U.H.) asked me another time, "Does he believe in what you believe?" I said, "No". He (P.B.U.H.) said, "O' Muyassir! Which part of earth is most valuable in the view of God?" I said, "Almighty God and his apostle and his progeny (P.B.U.T.) know better." The Imam (P.B.U.H.) said, "O' Muyassir! There is a garden of Heaven's gardens between *Rukn*[1] and *Maqām*[2] and also there is a garden of Heaven's gardens between the grave of the holy Prophet (P.B.U.H. & H.H.) and his rostrum. I Swear to God that if He gives a long lifetime to a servant and that servant prays to God between *Rukn* and *Maqām* and between the grave of the holy Prophet (P.B.U.H. & H.H.) and his podium for thousands of years and then he would be beheaded cruelly in his bed as a beautiful buck is beheaded, when he visits God (in the Hereafter) while he doesn't believe in our guardianship, God will throw him into Hell on his face."[3]

Therefore, the main condition of prayer being valid is acknowledgement of the guardianship of *Ahl al-Bayt* (P.B.U.T.). That is why in the presence of God, it isn't important how much one prayed to God but the point is

---

1. The eastern corner of *al-Ka'ba* on which *al-Ḥajar al-Aswad* (the Black Stone) is located.

2. The *Maqām Ibrāhīm* (Station of Abraham) is a stone associated with Abraham, Ishmael and their rebuilding of the *Ka'ba*.

3. Ṣadūq, M. (1406 A.H.), *Thawāb al-A'māl wa-'Iqāb al-A'māl*, Qom: Sharīf al-Raḍī, p. 210.

that *where* they established their prayer. According to the verses of *Sūra* Nūr, the place where one establishes their prayer has been highlighted, the location of worship has been emphasized and the place where one keeps the remembrance of God has been emphasized too. The holy shrines of *Ahl al-Bayt* (P.B.U.T.) are among these holy places and *Buyūt* (houses). The intended ultimate purpose of these houses, however, is the luminous existence of *Ahl al-Bayt* (P.B.U.T.) and their light of Imamate, guardianship and guidance that Almighty God has shed upon the world.

2. Considering the Shrines as Heaven

According to the traditions, the other authentic attitude toward the holy shrines of *Ahl al-Bayt* (P.B.U.T.) is the viewpoint of Heaven. If one enters the holy shrines of these dignitaries under the aegis of this attitude, and wholeheartedly believes that he has entered a garden of Heaven's gardens and is being pampered there, by this amount of cognition, undoubtedly he benefits a lot from this space.

Allah has said in the holy Qur'an,

سَيَهْدِيهِمْ وَيُصْلِحُ بَالَهُمْ * وَيُدْخِلُهُمُ الْجَنَّةَ عَرَّفَهَا لَهُمْ

He will guide them and set right their affairs * and admit them into
Paradise, with which He has acquainted them. (47: 5-6)

According to the above verses, in Heaven, the favors and blessings of God fall on the people of Heaven, and their affairs and matters settle greatly. Due to this fact, if the holy shrines of *Ahl al-Bayt* (P.B.U.T.) are a garden of Heaven's gardens, it should have these characteristics and qualities that according to the traditions, they have. But it depends who is entering under the aegis of this viewpoint and benefiting from these gardens.

So it is the result of this viewpoint that if one enters in Heaven, certainly he is well-served there and can make the most of this opportunity that Allah has given him and reform himself more than before and be a true Shiite and a soldier for *Ahl al-Bayt* (P.B.U.T.). Although many people's eyes can't see these shining and majestic gardens, they exist and are more beautiful and favorable than any other gardens and in the Hereafter when the veils are removed and the believers enter Heaven, they will testify that the favors being given to them right there, had been given to them in some similar gardens in the previous world.[1]

Ahl al-Bayt (P.B.U.T.) have implied this beautiful viewpoint through many traditions. Imam al-Ṣādiq (P.B.U.H.)

---

1. *The holy Qur'n, 2: 25,* "And give good news to those who have faith and do righteous deeds, that for them shall be gardens with streams running in them: whenever they are provided with their fruit for nourishment, they will say, 'This is what we were provided before,' and they were given something resembling it. There will be chaste mates for them, and they will remain therein [forever]."

says that the holy Prophet (P.B.U.H. & H.H.) stated, "There is a garden of Heaven's gardens between my house (this place is currently the grave of holy Prophet (P.B.U.H. & H.H.)) and my rostrum. My rostrum is located on a voluminous and elevated garden of lush and elevated gardens of Heaven and Almighty God has reared the bases of my rostrum in Heaven." Then he was asked, "Is here currently a garden of Heaven?" The holy Prophet (P.B.U.H. & H.H.) answered, "Yes! If the veil draws aside, you will see that here is a garden of Heaven's gardens."[1] Some of the historians and Shiite scholars have said about the holy and sacred grave of *Ḥaḍrat* Fāṭima (P.B.U.H.) that her holy tomb isn't in *Baqī'* cemetery, but it is between the tomb of the holy Prophet (P.B.U.H. & H.H.) and his rostrum and they have verified their claim utilizing another narration of this same *Ḥadīth* in which Imam al-Ṣādiq (P.B.U.H.) explicitly adds at the end the reason of this place being a garden of Heaven's gardens, and that's because here is the tomb of *Ḥaḍrat* Fāṭima (P.B.U.H.).[2]

It has also been said about the holy grave of Imam al-Riḍā (P.B.U.H.) that his holy grave is a garden of Heaven's gardens and one who comes to visit the tomb of Imam al-Riḍā (P.B.U.H.)–in fact–he has come to one of the garens of Heaven.[3] Hence one who goes to Mashhad to visit

---

1. *Al-Kāfī*, vol. 4, p. 554.
2. Ṣadūq, M. (1403 A.H.), *Ma'ānī al-Akhbār*, Qom: Daftar Intishārāt Islāmī, p. 267.
3. Ṣadūq, M. (1413 A.H.), *Man Lā Yaḥḍuruhū al-Faqīh*, Qom: Daftar Intishārāt Is-

Imam al-Riḍā (P.B.U.H.), he has actually entered in a garden of Heaven's gardens. The same thing has also been said about the holy grave of Imam al-Ḥussain (P.B.U.H.).[1]

Here, a question may be raised as to why most pilgrims are not able to see these magnificent and majestic gardens of Heaven which are full of blessings and favors. The answer is that it is due to the darkness of the world. As we know, nothing can be seen in a dark area and we are also in this dark world, and we go to visit Imam al-Riḍā (P.B.U.H.) and other *Ahl al-Bayt* (P.B.U.T.) in this world, so we don't feel those Heavenly gardens due to the materiality and darkness of this world. Yes, this world doesn't have enough light for us to see these gardens and Heaven isn't visible in this world. But as we proceed into the future and toward Heaven, that is located after this world, and as the veils are removed and more light glows, we can feel these favors more than before. We will discuss this matter in depth by talking about 'materialization of deeds' in the viewpoint of the 'Arsh.

In general, one of the acknowledged attitudes toward the holy shrines of the infallible Imams (P.B.U.T.) is the viewpoint of Heaven, and as the holy Prophet (P.B.U.H. &

---

lāmī, vol. 2, p. 585.

1. Imam Ṣādiq (P.B.U.H.) said, "The tomb of Imam Ḥusain (P.B.U.H.) has become a garden of Heaven's gardens since he was buried there."(*Al-Kāfī*, vol. 4, p. 588 and vol. 9, p. 347.)

H.H.) said, "The grave is either a garden of Heaven's gardens or a pit of Hell's pits."[1], the graves of all these dignitaries–who are the most honorable creatures–are undoubtedly gardens of Heaven's gardens.

3. Considering the Shrines as the Center of Sustenance and Decree

Based on verses of the holy Qur'an and the traditions of *Ahl al-Bayt* (P.B.U.T.) there is a night as the Night of Ordainment in which angels along with their superior "the Spirit" proffer the decrees of all creatures to the absolute supervisor of this universe. By the time the holy Prophet (P.B.U.H. & H.H.) was alive [life in its biological materialistic sense], all decrees were proffered to his majesty, but since then each Imam of the time was the Imam of the Night of Ordainment and received all decrees from the Spirit and the angels and endorsed them from God and now it is the time of the 12th Imam [Imam al-Mahdī] (May God hasten his advent) who is the Imam of the Night of Ordainment and the absolute supervisor of this universe. In a narrative, Imam al-Bāqir, Imam al-Ṣādiq, and Imam al-Kāẓim (P.B.U.T.) stated, "God, the Almighty, decrees all good and bad and what occurs durning the year at the Night of Ordainment. Also He includes His providence and what He wishes in it; He precedes and delays the destiny, provisions, security,

---

1. *Irshād al-Qulūb,* vol. 1. P. 74.

illness, health and etc., The holy Prophet (P.B.U.H. & H.H.) passed this mission [receiving all decrees from God] after himself to Imam 'Alī (P.B.U.H.) and so did his majesty to the Imams (P.B.U.T.) until it is Imam al-Mahdī's (May God hasten his advent) period."[1]

In other words, at every Night of Ordainment, all decrees and orders are passed to the living Imam of every time[2] by angels from God and the Imam endorses them by God's permission and after the end of each year there is another Night of Ordainment and these nights are repeated every year and this would continue "until the emergence of the *dawn*".[3]

If we look at the Imams (P.B.U.T.) from the viewpoint of 'the Imams of the Night of Ordainment', we see them as those who receive and deliever not only all our decrees but also the decrees of the whole universe in one year by God's permission.

Sublime God states,

1. Majlisī, M. B. (1403 A.H.), *Biḥār al-Anwār al-Jāmi'ah li-Durar Akhbār al-A'immat al-Aṭhār*, Beirut: Dār Iḥyā' al-Turāth al-'Arabī, vol. 4, p. 101.
2. Imam Ṣādiq (A), "In the Night of Decree, the details of all events are sent to the absolute supervisor and he is ordered too what to do about himself and about people."(*Al-Kāfī*, vol. 1, p.248.)
3. Here is the complete translation of *Ṣūra al-Ghadr*, "Indeed We sent it down on the Night of Ordainment. (1) And what will show you what is the Night of Ordainment? (2) The Night of Ordainment is better than a thousand months. (3) In it the angels and the Spirit descend, by the leave of their Lord, with every command. (4) It is peaceful until the rising of the dawn. (5)."

وَ فِي السَّماءِ رِزْقُكُمْ وَ ما تُوعَدُونَ

And in the sky is your provision and what you are promised.

(51: 22)

Here, the question is that who brings all these yearly sustenance down to earth in a year. In response to this question we shall say: according to the traditions of *Ahl al-Bayt* (P.B.U.T.), the Imam of every time would receive these decrees at the Night of Ordainment from the Holy Spirit, and then endorses them, irrespective of what they are, whether Karbala event or the food portion of a tiny creature in the depths of oceans. But who or what makes the decrees be descended and exerted along the year? Although it is God's Will that decrees be descended and applied consecutively, it requires a mechanism, a reason, and what would that be? In *Al-Kāfī* it is stated from Imam al-Ṣādiq (P.B.U.H.) that he said, "God refuses to do things without [their] reasons; that is why for everything He placed a reason! ...; those reasons are the Prophet and we *Ahl al-Bayt* (P.B.U.T.)."[1]

So the reason that makes connection between the sky and the earth, brings down the orders decreed in the sky at the Night of Ordainment year by year, and exerts them by God's permission is *Ahl al-Bayt* (P.B.U.T.). Also in *Nudbah prayer*, Imam al-Mahdī (May God hasten his advent) is described as this,

---

1. *Al-Kāfī*, vol. 1, p.183.

أَيْنَ السَّبَبُ الْمُتَّصِلُ بَيْنَ الأَرْضِ و السَّماء

Where is the means of access that is connectedly extended between
the earth and the heavens?[1]

This viewpoint is a highly celestial perspective and can revolutionize our visit to the holy shrines of *Ahl al-Bayt* (P.B.U.T.). Blessed with such attitude, we observe them as the ones that the pilgrim's affairs are in their hands by God's permission. Thus, in their holy shrines where is the center of any Divine Decree and any heavenly sustenance, the pilgrim sees his works apt to reform and thus utilizes his chance of pilgrimage and asks the Imam of the Night of Ordainment, "My lord, the Night of Ordainment and the decree and the sustenance is in your powerful hands, indulge us and reform our works and endorse the best of decrees for us and omit negative and wasteful issues in the new year."

4. Considering the Shrines as the *'Arsh* (The Divine Throne)

The other viewpoint that the pilgrims can have toward the holy shrines of *Ahl al-Bayt* (P.B.U.T.) is the perspective of *'Arsh*. In this regard, it has been narrated that one day the holy Prophet (P.B.U.H. & H.H.) was in the house of *Ḥaḍrat* Fāṭima (P.B.U.H.), and Imam 'Alī, Imam al-Ḥasan and Imam

---

1. Qumī, 'A. (2010 A.H.), *Mafātīḥ al-Jinān* (Badr Shahin trans.), Qom: Ansariyan, vol. 2, p. 741.

al-Ḥussain (P.B.U.T.) were beside him and all of them were very happy and joyful. At this moment, the trustworthy Gabriel (P.B.U.H.) came down and said, "O' Muḥammad! Allah grants peace and honor to you and says, "Are you happy to be with your family?" The holy Prophet (P.B.U.H. & H.H.) replied, "Yes! And I thank God because of this gathering." Gabriel (P.B.U.H.) said, "These honorable people will be killed and their graves will be dispersed and scattered." After hearing this news, the holy Prophet of mercy (P.B.U.H. & H.H.) wept extremely until Imam ʿAlī (P.B.U.H.) said to him, "O' Messenger of Allah! Why are you weeping?" The holy Prophet (P.B.U.H. & H.H.) said, "O' ʿAlī (P.B.U.H.)! Gabriel has informed me of your future and says all of you will be killed and your graves will be dispersed." Imam ʿAlī (P.B.U.H.) said, "Praise be to God due to the sorrows He has devoted to us." Then he said, "What is the reward of the one who visits us during our lifetime or after our death and martyrdom?" The holy Prophet (P.B.U.H. & H.H.) replied, "O' ʿAlī (P.B.U.H.)! Whoever visits me or you, or Fāṭima, or Ḥasan, or Ḥussain (P.B.U.T.) during our lifetime or after death, is like the one who has visited Allah, the Almighty, on His Throne and Allah will write the reward of the one who struggles in His path." Imam ʿAlī (P.B.U.H.) said, "Praise be to God due to this blessing He has devoted to us."[1]

---

1. Ibn Abī Jumhūr al-Aḥsāʾī, M. (1405 A.H.), *ʿAwāli al-Laʾālī al-ʿazīzīyya fī al-Aḥādīth al-Dīnīyya*, Qom: Dār Sayyid al-Shuhadā, vol. 4, p. 83.

We have already discussed in this book traditions with the same meaning which assert that the visit of Imam al-Riḍā and Imam al-Ḥussain (P.B.U.T.) is equal to the vist of Allah on His Throne.[1]

Therefore, the viewpoint of the Divine Throne is one of the attitudes that the progeny of the holy Prophet (P.B.U.T.) used to consider and express for themselves. This means that when the pilgrim moves toward the holy shrines of these dignitaries or even when he intends to visit one of the *Ahl al-Bayt* (P.B.U.T.) until he arrives to their holy shrines, he should keep his mind on this matter that he is going to visit the Throne of God and during his whole travel, he must remember that he is walking on the Divine Throne and soaring toward it.

The holy Prophet (P.B.U.H. & H.H.) has stated, "Surely, Almighty God created us when there was no earth and sky, no Paradise and Hell, no *Lawḥ* (the Tablet) and *Qalam* (the Pen)[2]; when He wanted to create us, He said a word which transformed into a light! Then He said another word that changed into the Spirit and–afterwards–He mixed them and created me and 'Alī (P.B.U.H.) from that, and then He created *'Arsh* (the Throne) out of my light, therefore, I am more glorious than the Divine Throne, and He created the skies from the light of 'Alī (P.B.U.H.), hence, 'Alī (P.B.U.H.) is

---

1. *Kāmil al-Zīyārāt*, p. 147. *Al-Kāfī*, vol.4, p. 585.
2. *Lawḥ* and *Qalam* are Qur'anic words, see: 85: 22; 61: 1.

more glorious than the skies, and He created the sun from the light of Ḥasan (P.B.U.H.) and then He created the moon from the light of Ḥussain (P.B.U.H.), so Ḥasan and Ḥussain (P.B.U.T.) are more magnificent than the sun and the moon.[1]. There are many traditions approving the same concept that the 'Arsh is a light from the lights of Ahl al-Bayt (P.B.U.T.)[2].

When a person looks at Ahl al-Bayt (P.B.U.T.) through the perspective of the 'Arsh, he sees that the dignitary whom he wants to visit isn't just the owner of the tomb! but–in fact–he is the light of God, a light which all the creation has been originated from and everything has been created out of its light, a light which is greatly superior to the Divine 'Arsh, because this light is located on top of the Divine 'Arsh, and the Divine 'Arsh has been created from it. According to this perspective, the *height* of the holy shrines of Ahl al-Bayt (P.B.U.T.) is greatly further than the skies up to the Divine 'Arsh.

Therefore, when we go to the holy shrines of the Infallibles (P.B.U.T.), we shouldn't suppose that we have come to a material place! Or we have come to visit a tomb! But we should imagine that we have come to the presence of

---

1. *Irshad al-Ghulūb*, vol2. P. 403.
2. For instance, see: Khaṣībī, Ḥ., (1377 A.H. (solar)), *Al-Hidāyat Al-Kubrā*, Beirut: Al-Balāq, vol. 1, p. 392; *Al-Burhān fī Tafsīr al-Qur'an*, vol. 5, p. 145; *Biḥār al-Anwār*, vol. 36, p.73.

a light which is located on top of the Divine *'Arsh.* How great and high is the *'Arsh*? Extremely high! It is extremely higher than the farthest stars, much higher than the skies!

Materialization of deeds

An important question may arise here as to why, in spite of all these excellent and worthy interpretations in relation to the holy shrines of the infallible Imams (P.B.U.T.), most of the people can't feel these favors and descriptions in the material world. Is it correct to consider these favors and descriptions symbolic and as a mere allegory due to the fact that they aren't visible or tangible?

The answer is: No! According to the *materialization of deeds* (or *the embodiment of deeds* or *the representation of deeds*), all the punishments and rewards, favors and disfavors, afflictions and torments, as well as the happiness and gladness of the Hereafter and so on, all and all are the realities of our worldly actions and intentions that will represent themselves and become visible at that time. There are many verses in the holy Qur'an concerning the materialization[1], and from them it is inferred that any act or intention has another form which is hidden from the eyes of mankind, but when the curtains are removed in

---

1. For instance: 3: 30, 2: 174, 4: 10.

the other world, the hidden facts will be apparent. The holy Qur'an says,

$$يَوْمَ تُبْلَى السَّرائِرُ$$

On the day when the secrets are examined. (86: 9)

Thereupon the Day of Judgment will reveal this fact and all people will know that the holy shrines of *Ahl al-Bayt* (P.B.U.T.) are the real, elegant, glorious, merciful and the shiny *thrones* and the Divine '*Arsh*. The Day of Judgment will show the fact that the one who went to visit these dignitaries, in fact, had walked on top of the Throne and the owner of this house was a person who had been placed on the Divine '*Arsh* and,

$$يومَ يُكشَفُ عَن ساقٍ$$

The day when the pillars of His Throne will be visible. (68: 42)

When the Divine Throne will be unveiled, all people will be able to see that, in the Day of Judgment, the Divine Throne is the actual position of *Ahl al-Bayt* (P.B.U.T.).

Imam Jaʿfar al-Ṣādiq (P.B.U.H.) has said in a long quotation, "When the Day of Judgment is set, Almighty God will resurrect the creatures as He had created them for the first time and will gather them again." And on that occasion the Imam (P.B.U.H.) said, "Then it will be our turn and we will come to our real position and sit on the Throne of our God. Then the books (Dossier of deeds of every person) will be brought to us and set up. At that moment, we will be witness to our enemies and intercessor for our sinful friends and followers."[1]

Thus, in spite of the fact that this world is dark and limited and these factors don't let us see the real qualities of these holy shrines, but when the Day of Judgment is set, the visit that a pilgrim has made in the holy shrine of Imam al-Riḍā (P.B.U.H.) or in the holy shrine of Imam al-Ḥussain (P.B.U.H.) or in the holy shrines of other *Ahl al-Bayt* (P.B.U.T.) will be materialized in the form of walking on top of the Divine Throne and soaring toward the realm of God's *'Arsh*, and that visit will be equal to visiting the Throne of Allah and being on it.

---

1. 'Ayyāshī, M. (1380 A.H.), *Tafsīr Al-'Ayyashī*, Tehran: al-Matba'a al-'Elmīyyah, vol. 2, p. 310.

Viewpoints about the Pilgrimage to Ahl al-Bayt's (P.B.U.T.) Shrines

This issue has considerable importance and can help us be benefited from the light of these dignitaries. It means how one can see oneself comparing to these dignitaries at the time of going to visit their holy shrines and according to that perspective, what kind of thoughts and behaviors they may have toward these holy persons and shrines.

Here are some viewpoints and attitudes that a pilgrim can have toward *Ahl al-Bayt* (P.B.U.T.) at the time of visiting their holy shrines.

1. The Pilgrim as a Supplicant

يَاأَيُّهَا النَّاسُ أَنْتُمُ الْفُقَرَاءُ إِلَى اللَّهِ وَ اللَّهُ هُوَ الْغَنِيُّ الْحَمِيدُ

O' mankind !You are the ones who stand in need of Allah,and Allah—
He is the All-sufficient ,the All-laudable (35 :15) .

The viewpoint of being a supplicant is one of the attitudes that a pilgrim can have toward the infallibles (P.B.U.T.) at the time of their visit or perhaps at all times. According to this verse and based on the true monotheism, in front of Almighty God and His successors, we are like the supplicants located before a king. We are like the insistent beggars who have gone to the door of a generous king and constantly cry and implore him; they continually repent and make requests from him. We should consider the progeny of the holy Prophet (P.B.U.T.) as our king and behave in a way that shows the condition of a beggar located in the presence of a king.

'Alī b. Asbāṭ has narrated that, "In the Day of 'Arafa, I went to see and visit the holy essence of Imam al-Riḍā (P.B.U.H.). When I entered his house, I sat down and after a while he addressed me and said, "Prepare my horse so that we can go outside." When I got the horse ready, he mounted it and then he set out for Baqī' graveyard to visit the holy grave of his noble mother, Lady Fāṭima (P.B.U.H.), and I accompanied the holy essence of Imam al-Riḍā (P.B.U.H.). When we entered Baqī' graveyard, I said to him, "O' my master and protector! To whom should I say Salam? He said, "Say Salam to Lady Fāṭima, Ḥasan and Ḥussain, 'Alī b. al-Ḥussain, Muḥammad b. 'Alī, Jafar b. Muḥammad, and Mūsa b. Ja'far, the best benedictions and the most complete salutations be upon them." So I gave compliments and Salam to each of those infallible dignitaries and we came back home. On the way back, I said: "O' the son of the holy Prophet (P.B.U.H & H.H.)! O' my dear master and protector! I am in need and have nothing to give to my family as a gift in 'Īd al-'Aḍḥā to make them happy and glad on this day. After hearing my words and request, the gracious Imam (P.B.U.H.) immediately drew a line on the earth with his cane and then bent down and picked up a piece of gold that its value was nearly one hundred dinars and gave it to me. When I got that valuable gift from him, I became happy and could meet the needs of my family and myself."[1]

In *Amīn Allah* statement of tribute that has been highly recommended to be recited at the time of observing the holy shrines of Imams (P.B.U.T.) we say to God in the presence of these sacred dignaraties,

وَجَوَآئِزَ السَّآئِلِينَ عِنْدَك مُوَفَّرَةٌ وَ عَوَآئِدَ الْمَزِيدِ مُتَواتِرَةٌ

And the prizes of those begging You are offered, and Your gifts for further conferrals are uninterrupted.[2]

Yes, these holy kings welcome the beggars of their house in this way and greet them with kindness.

2. The Pilgrim as a Traveler

The other efficient viewpoint that one can have toward the holy shrines of *Ahl al-Bayt* (P.B.U.T.) is the perspective of being a traveler. When a faithful person wants to travel, firstly, he makes an ablution and tries to prepare himself through putting his reliance upon God. He also provides

---

1. Ibn Ḥamza Ṭūsī, M. (1419 A.H.), *Al-Thāqib fi al-Manāqib*, Qom: Ansariyan, p. 473.
2. Al-Shahīd al-Awwal, M. (1410 A.H.), *Al-Mazār fī kayfiyyati zīyārāt al-Nabī wa al-Aʾimma*, Qom: Madrasa Imām al-Mahdī, p. 116.

some provisions for his journey; therefore he organizes his affairs and carries out his postponed works. He pays off all his debts and altogether he makes some arrangements and then he goes on a trip.

When someone wants to travel, he completely prepares himself for that and takes all the necessary and even unnecessary precautions, for example at the time of leaving, the button of his shirt isn't open or the laces of his shoes aren't unfastened to cause him any trouble. During the travel, he tries to observe some habits so that he would be able to have a good and beneficial trip. Likewise, in this world a faithful person constantly seeks the requirements for the long journey toward the Hereafter, a journey toward God, a journey in which he should collect provisions as much as he can, and he is frightened by the difficult events ahead of himself and thus he needs the Divine Mercy. According to this verse,

يَا أَيُّهَا الْإِنْسَانُ إِنَّكَ كَادِحٌ إِلَى رَبِّكَ كَدْحًا فَمُلَاقِيهِ

O man! You are labouring toward your Lord laboriously, and you will encounter Him. (84: 6)

the path which goes toward God is a difficult path; that's why Imam 'Alī (P.B.U.H.) cries and sighs during his supplication and says,

O', how little is the provision, how long the path, how distant the journey, and how splendid the destination.[1]

Therefore, a traveler is always prepared and ready to go.

For a pilgrim, the journey of pilgrimage is a journey in which he has the same spirit as a traveler and he finds himself in the atmosphere of departure, he is free from this world and has set his heart on the journey. When such a person arrives at the presence of the Imams (P.B.U.T.), instead of asking them for the worldly affairs and needs, he tries to get the provision of his long and difficult journey to the other world, he gets the expenses of his journey and asks them for a power to move and supplicates to them for perfection, security and happiness. He is looking for the most lightweight and rich provision which isn't possible to be achieved except with the help of these dignitaries who are the treasurers of the whole universe.

A person who goes to visit the holy shrines of *Ahl al-Bayt* (P.B.U.T.) using the attitude of a traveler has the least attention to jewels and fineries and the exterior parts of the holy shrines and the worldly affairs. He draws all of his attention to his constant companions–the Imams of the whole universe–because during his long path and difficult journey toward God and the future, no one can accompany him and take on the leadership of his caravan

---

1. Al-Sharīf al-Raḍī, M. (1414 A.H.), *Nahj al-Balāghah* (research by Ṣubḥī Ṣāliḥ), Qom: Hejirah, p. 481.

except them–the only ones who can bring the best ending to his journey.

3. The Pilgrim as a Guest

The other viewpoint that pilgrims can have toward the holy shrines of *Ahl al-Bayt* (P.B.U.T.) is the attitude of a guest. It means that one regards himself as a guest who has sat near the blessed and blissful table of his merciful protector and believes that the merciful Imam will respectfully receive him.

The holy Prophet (P.B.U.H. & H.H.) said,

> Whoever believes in Allah and the Last Day must respectfully receive his guest. [1]

According to this matter, *Ahl al-Bayt* (P.B.U.T.) are the main purpose of this narrative, because they are the real believers, and thus they are those who respectfully receive and welcome their guests.

Who is a better host than the benevolent family of the Prophet (P.B.B.T.)? They will kindly recognize the right of their guests and constantly welcome and respect them and pay attention to their needs. What an unbelievable grace from God to this guest!

---

1. *Al-Kāfī*, vol.2, p. 667.

We read in *Zīyārat* of Imam al-Ḥasan and Imam al-Ḥussain (P.B.U.T.) on Mondays, "On this day, I am your guest; therefore, receive me as your guest and treat me hospitably. Verily, you both are the most excellent hosts a guest may gain."[1]

4. The Pilgrim as a Friend

God, the Almighty, has said in the holy Qur'an,

وَمَن يُطِع اللَّـهَ وَالرَّسُولَ فَأُولَـٰئِكَ مَعَ الَّذِينَ أَنْعَمَ اللَّـهُ عَلَيْهِم مِّنَ النَّبِيِّينَ وَالصِّدِّيقِينَ وَالشُّهَدَاءِ وَالصَّالِحِينَ وَحَسُنَ أُولَـٰئِكَ رَفِيقًا

Whoever obeys Allah and the Apostle—they are with those whom Allah has blessed ,including the prophets and the truthful ,the martyrs and the righteous ,and excellent companions are they (4:64)

The holy Prophet (P.B.U.H. & H.H.) has said that the last part (حَسُنَ أُولئِکَ رَفِیقاً: and excellent companions are they) refers to the twelve Imams who would come after him (P.B.U.T.).[2]

When a person goes to the holy shrines of these dignitaries, if he considers them as the kings of the world and wholeheartedly believes in it, then he should grab a *Zīyārat Nāmih* (a booklet written in Arabic which contains prayers, supplications, special texts for *Zīyārah*, and other texts that are recommended to be read or recited

---

1. *Mafātīḥ al-Jinān*, vol. 1, pp. 197-198.
2. Ibn Shahrāshūb, M. (1379 A.H.), *Manāqib Āli Abī Ṭālib*, Qom: 'Allāma, vol. 1, p. 283.

at the time of visiting the holy shrines) and will shake with fear and modestly read the *Zīyārat Nāmeh* in a formal manner before them and then bow down to them and go out of there, lest the kings should be offended. But if he believes in the fact that *Ahl al-Bayt* (P.B.U.T.), although being the kings of the universe, deal with their followers and pilgrims in a kindly way, then when he arrives there, he greets them as his friends and companions and says, "Salam; how are you? I have really missed you".

He talks to the visited Imam and if he can't kiss the holy face of Imam, he kisses his holy shrine and every tiny part of it, calmly sits in a corner, and then leans against the wall without straightening his leg and misbehaving, he heaves a deep sigh and says, "O' my master! You have got a splendid holy shrine, although I know you aren't interested in this world and that you love a simple and ordinary life. Well, O my master! Are you okay? I have really missed you. O my master! It is the custom for a friend to spread a tablecloth for his friend and I'm sure that you have already spread the tablecloth for me, a tablecloth filled with affection and favors and graces."

A friend should give his whole attention to his friend, and *Ahl al-Bayt* (P.B.U.T.), who are the best friends throughout the world constantly, pay all their attention to their companions and friends.

Some of the letters from Imam al-Mahdī (May God hasten his advent) to al-Shaykh al-Mufīd were titled as "to my dear and firm brother, al-Shaykh al-Mufīd."[1]

It has also been narrated from Sayyid b. Ṭāwūs that one morning, in the holy basement of Imam al-Mahdī(May God hasten his advent),[2] he heard this invocation from the Imam,

O' God! Our followers (Shiites) have been created through the beam of our light and from the rest of our nature. They have committed a lot of sins relying upon our affection and guardianship. If their sins are relevant to you, forgive them and please us through it, and if they are related to themselves and other people, correct their relationships yourself ... and save them from the Hellfire and differentiate between them and our enemies and don't become angry with them.[3]

Hence *Ahl al-Bayt* (P.B.U.T.) always pay attention to their followers. It has been stated in the traditions that at the time of *Ẓohūr* (the advent of Imam al-Mahdī (May God hasten his advent)), the Imam treats his followers and companions with affection and in a friendly manner and that is the time when a friend never forgets his friend. In prayer *Nudbah*, we supplicate to God for this matter and say,

---

1. For instance, see, *Al-Iḥtijāj*, vol. 2, p.497.
2. It is located in Samarra in the western part of the holy shrine of Imam 'Askarī and Imam Hādī (P.B.U.T.).
3. *Biḥār al-Anwār*, vol.53, pp. 302.

Establish, O Allah, between him and us a connection that leads us
to accompany his ancestors,[1]

They are the very *excellent companions* we already mentioned from
the holy Qur'an (4: 69).

At the time of *Ahl al-Bayt* (P.B.U.T.), some would consider
the Imam of the time as the successor of God; one would
look at him as a master of mystics; another person would
see him as a king and the other would assume that he is
the one who should be given the *Khums* and *Zakāt* (a fixed
part of the wealth of a Muslim that should be given as an
obligatory charity). Among these points of views, there
were few people who treated their Imam as a friend.

For example, when Jābir b. ʿAbdullāh Anṣārī came to
Karbala a few days after the incident of *ʿĀshūrā*, he treated Imam al-Ḥussain (P.B.U.H.) in a friendly manner. He was
blind at that time and according to another account, he
went blind after that. He came to Karbala along with a
man named ʿAtīya ʿAwfī. ʿAtīya says, "We came to visit the
tomb of Imam al-Ḥussain (P.B.U.H.). When we arrived in
Karbala, Jābir went to Furat River and performed *Ghusl*
(major ablution) and wore new clothes… When he came
to the grave of Imam al-Ḥussain (P.B.U.H.), he unconscious-
ly threw himself on the grave. I poured some water over
his face. When he became conscious, he cried, "Yā Ḥus-

---

1. *Mafātīḥ al-Jinān*, vol.2, p. 751.

sain! Yā Ḥussain! Yā Ḥussain!" And afterwards he said, "a friend who doesn't answer his friend".[1]

Also, after the burial ceremony of Imam 'Alī (P.B.U.H.) and on the way back to Kufa, Imam al-Ḥasan (P.B.U.H.) and his companions noticed a sound coming out of a ruin; they went over there and saw that a blind old man is invocating and crying. They said to him, "O' old man! What do you want?" He answered, "Nothing." They asked him, "Do you want some food?" "No, I'm not crying for food", he answered. "So what is the problem?" they asked. He began to explain, "I'm a blind beggar, an old man who has no family and relatives; I had a friend who used to come to me late at night and sit near me. He would talk to me and pour out his heart to me; he was my friend and always asked me about my condition. But he hasn't come here for two or three nights, I have sorely missed my friend." They asked him, "O' the old man! What did your friend look like? How was he?" "I'm blind and I haven't seen his face", he answered. They asked the old man to tell them about the attributes and the behaviors of his friend and when that old man described the attributes of his friend, Imam al-Ḥasan (P.B.U.H.) said, "He was the Chief of the Faithful (P.B.U.H.), our father, and now we are coming back from his funeral!" That old man had neither eyes nor

---

1. 'Imād al-Dīn al-Tabarī, M. (1383 A.H.), *Bishārat al-Muṣṭafā li Shī'at al-Murtaḍā*, Najaf: Heydarīya Pub., p. 74.

any possession in the world. He used to live at the corner of a ruin, but he had the Chief of the Faithful (P.B.U.H.). Imam ʿAlī (P.B.U.H.) was in possession of him. But now he had lost all his wealth and possession. He asked Imam al-Ḥasan (P.B.U.H.) to take him to Imam ʿAlī's grave. When he arrived, he cried so much and prayed to God that "I cannot tolerate this disaster and no longer want to be alive". Unbelievably, his prayer was immediately answered and then he was buried beside his dearest friend, the Chief of the Faithful (P.B.U.H.).[1]

This perspective has a great impact on our behavoiur as pilgrims of the holy shrines of *Ahl al-Bayt* (P.B.U.T.) and can automatically lead and help us to gain the conduct which is admired by them. Friendship is so much impressive on the beliefs and behavior that the holy Prophet (P.B.U.H. & H.H.) has stated,

Man holds up to the faith of his friend! Thus, take care whom you make friends with [2]

The chief of the faithful (P.B.U.H.) also said to Kumayl, "Your friend is your faith! So, take care of your faith as far as you can."[3]

---

1. Muhammadi Ishtihardi, M., (1381 A.H. (solar)), *Dastan Dustan*, Qom: Bustan Kitab, vol. 5, p. 203.
2. Ṭūsī, M. (1414 A.H.), *Al-Amālī*, Qum: Dar Al-Thiqāfa, vol.1, p. 518.
3. Ibid., p. 110.

5. The Pilgrim as a Child

Parents, in lower levels than God and *Ahl al-Bayt* (P.B.U.T.), have the utmost love, benevolence and sympathy for their children. They are ready to sacrifice their lives for their children's comfort. Parents consider their children as the greatest fruits of life. When the children reach the toddler years, they protect them with their life, provide them with all possible facilities necessary for their peace, comfort and health. In their teens, the parents prepare the grounds of education and growth for them and refrain from enjoing their own personal pleasures. They are as sympathetic gardeners who don't come short a single moment to see their children's hardship.

As a result, children have great responsibilities toward their parents. According to the holy Qur'an and the narratives of *Ahl al-Bayt* (P.B.U.T.), after God and His honorable successors (P.B.U.T.), children must obey their parents and respect them and show mercy to them. For example,

"Your Lord has decreed that you shall not worship anyone except Him, and [He has enjoined] kindness to parents." (17: 23)

Numerous traditions also explain the importance of attention to parents and the big responsibility toward them. Here is one example: a young person came to the Prophet (P.B.U.H & H.H.) and said that he is so greedy about Jihad, but his old parents needed his presence and help. The Prophet (P.B.U.H & H.H.) said, "I swear to God that a full day service to them is worth more than a year waging Jihad."[1]

Ahl al-Bayt (P.B.U.T.) As the Kindest Parents

As mentioned above, children have great obligations and duties toward their parents, however our real parents are *Ahl al-Bayt* (P.B.U.T.) who are above our biological parents and we have much greater and more tremendous duties toward them comparing to the natural parents.

In a narrative, the Chief of the Faithful (P.B.U.H.) said, "I heard the holy Prophet (P.B.U.H. & H.H.) saying, "'Alī and I are the fathers of this nation [*Umma*] and our rights are much greater than the biological fathers and if our children follow us, we will save them from Hell and send them to Heaven and will grant them freedom from slavery."[2]

Explaining these two verses, "And what will show you what is the Night of Ordainment? The Night of Ordainment is better than a thousand months." (97: 2-3), Imam al-Ṣādiq (P.B.U.H.) said, "Lady Fāṭima (P.B.U.H.) is superior to a thousand of faithful Muslims since she is the *'umm al-mu'minīn*, the mother of all faithful Muslims."[3]

---

1. *Al-Kāfī*, vol.2, p. 160.
2. *Biḥār al-Anwār*, vol.23, p. 259.
3. Kūfī, F., (1410 A.H.), *Tafsīr Furāt al-Kūfī*, Tehran: Ministry of Islamic Guidance Pub., p. 581.

And in addition, Imam al-Riḍā (P.B.U.H.) has stated that an infallible Imam is "a trustworthy friend, a kind father, a sympathetic mother toward her little baby, and a shelter for those who believe in God from awesome and frightening dangers."[1]

From all these statements it can be inferred that the holy Prophet and the Chief of the Faithful along with all infallible Imams (P.B.U.T.) are as the fathers of this nation and *Haḍrat* Zahrā (P.B.U.H.) is a mother kinder than any mother for faithful believers and all pure souls.

Parents love their children and worry about them; and in the case of *Ahl Al-Bayt* (P.B.U.T.), the parents are infallible and the children are sinful, the parents are divine and the children are sunken in murk, the parents live as saints and the children as sinners. Who are the children of Imam ʿAlī (P.B.U.H.)? They are the pure souls, lovers, devotees, Shiites and followers. Apart from these complaisant children, however, there are some sinful children who are in trouble and need the parents' help and support more than others. In this case, a father won't let his children remain in Hell though he himself is in Heaven and saved. Therefore, he carries the burden of his children's sins and the holy Prophet (P.B.U.H. & H.H.) will include these sins too in his account, so as for their honor in the presence of

---

1. *Al-Kāfī*, vol.1, p. 198.

God, God would forgive them[1]. That is why the Chief of the Faithful (P.B.U.H.) in *Kumayl Prayer* asks God for forgiveness of the sins we all know that he has not committed or even intended to do at all, and says,

اللَّهُمَ اغْفِرْلِيَ الذُّنُوبَ الَّتِي تَهْتِكُ الْعِصَمَ

O Allah, forgive me those sins which tear apart safeguards!

اللَّهُمَ اغْفِرْ لِيَ الذُّنُوبَ الَّتِي تُنْزِلُ النِّقَمَ

O Allah ,forgive me those sins which draw down adversities!

[and also the sins which block prayers and so on][2]...

As for our mother, Ḥaḍrat Fāṭima (P.B.U.H.), we should notice that the name "Fāṭima" means that God has withdrawn her and whoever loves her from Hellfire[2], and such a sympathetic mother wouldn't allow her children burning in fire; so then she will be there taking her Shiites and devotees from the wilderness of the Day of Judgment and its hellacious atmosphere and will lead them to Heaven.

As a result, *Ahl al-Bayt* (P.B.U.T.) are our kind parents and in response to all our impoliteness, mistakes and sins, they behave kindly and patiently.

---

1. Imam Ṣādiq said that the Prophet told Imam 'Ali (P.B.U.T.), "God has put all your followers' sins in my account and then has forgiven them for my sake and that's what God says, "That God may forgive your former and future sins" (48: 2). (*Ma 'ānī al-Akhbār*, p. 352.)

2. Imam Riḍā quotes from the Prophet (P.B.U.T.) as saying, "Verily I named my daughter Fāṭima because the Honorable and the Exalted God has withdrawn her and withdrawn whoever loves her from Helfire." (Ṣadūq, M., (1378 A.H.), *'Uyūn Akhbār al-Riḍā* (P.B.U.H.), Tehran: Jahān, vol. 2, p. 46.)

Once a man from *Shām* (Syria) arrived in Medina. He was not wicked deep in his heart, but had a severe grudge against Imam ʿAlī (P.B.U.H.) and his children due to the propaganda of *Muʿāwīya* and the other enemies of *Ahl al-Bayt* (P.B.U.T.). While he was walking down the streets of the city, he noticed a horseman who was being respected and greeted by the pedestrians as they were moving out of his way. The man approached and asked, "Who is this man you are respecting so much?" They replied, "He is Ḥasan (P.B.U.H.) the son of ʿAlī (P.B.U.H.)." Hearing that, he went frowningly to Imam al-Ḥasan (P.B.U.H.). He stood before him and started scolding and insulting him and his father as much as he could. But Imam (P.B.U.H.) waited until he finished insulting, then smiled and started like this, "You old man, I guess you are a stranger, sounds you are mistaken; now if you would ask for pardon we would forgive you, if you would need anything we would grant you, if you wish for guidance we would guide you, if you would need a ride we would give you, if you are hungry we would feed you, if you have no clothes to wear we would provide you with clothes, if you are poor we would pay you, if you are expelled from your home we would shelter you, and now you better take your things to my house and live with us until the end of your trip, because my house is spacious and all accommodations are set...." Imam's tender words went through the man's heart while the beads of teardrops blocked his sight.

The kind Imam's words finished and the man, his eyes full of tears, said, "I attest that you [and your family] are God's vicegerent[s] on earth and, for certain, God knows better to whom He should give His vicegerency. Before we met here, you and your father (Imam 'Alī (P.B.U.H.)) were my greatest enemies, but now I assume no one is as lovely as you."[1]

Yes, this is the behavior of the infallible and kind Imams (P.B.U.T.) that is more compassionate than all parents, and God has bestowed upon us such an eternal grace and blessing. If human beings look at themselves as the children of *Ahl al-Bayt* (P.B.U.T.), they would feel a strong earnest love for *Ahl al-Bayt* (P.B.U.T.), they will be embarrassed to displease these holy majesties and to dirty their holy shrines with gross deeds.

6. The Pilgrim as a Hajji

Respecting this viewpoint, it is mentioned in traditions that *Ka'ba* is an example of an Imam or an Imam is an example of *Ka'ba* which is acceptable on both sides.[2] Such traditions signify that if you see *Ka'ba*, it would resemble

---

1. *Biḥār al-Anwār,* vol. 43, p. 344.
2. The holy Prophet (P.B.U.H. & H.H.) said, "Imam is like *Ka'ba,* since it is refered to and never refers to any one." (Shaykh Hurr al-'Āmilī, M., (1425 A.H.), *Ithbāt al-hudāt bi al-Nuṣūṣ wa al-Mu'jizāt,* Beirut: A'lamī, vol. 3, p. 117.) It is also narrated that once Gabriel came to the Pophet and said, "'Alī is like *Ka'ba* that people aim at but he never aims at anybody." (Ṭabarī al-Ṣaghīr, M., (1413 A.H.), *Dalā'il al-Imāma,* Qom: Bi'that, p. 82.)

the Imams or vice versa; the Imams are the example of *Ka'ba*, signifying that, "O' Muslims! We should respect and treat them the same as *Ka'ba*."

Hajj: Behavior toward the Holy Prophet's Successors (P.B.U.T.)

From the initial years of *Bi'tha*, the holy Prophet (P.B.U.H. & H.H.), among his all supporters and followers spoke about his successor clearly in various ways and wordings. How many great occasions in which Imam 'Alī (P.B.U.H.) was introduced by the Prophet (P.B.U.H. & H.H.) as his successor or what glorious titles which were granted to him, so as to make every one understand if there is a successor, he is no one but 'Alī–the son of Abū Ṭālib–the Chief of the Faithful (P.B.U.H.).

Among all that was stated by the holy Prophet (P.B.U.H. & H.H.) about the Chief of the Faithful (P.B.U.H.), the example of *Ka'ba* sparks more brightly. After all explications introducing *Ahl al-Bayt* (P.B.U.T.) as *Ka'ba* and all instructions for people to resort to them while performing Hajj, his majesty (P.B.U.H. & H.H.) in the practical class of the *Ḥajjat al-Wadā'* or *farewell Hajj*[1], took a big number of Muslims to Hajj and in the end, introduced the living *Ka'ba*–Imam 'Alī

---

1. The last Hajj of the holy Prophet (P.B.U.H. & H.H.) and his only Hajj after Hejira that occurred in 10 A.H., a few months before his demise.

(P.B.U.H.)–as his successor and the leader of all mankind and universe. The Prophet (P.B.U.H. & H.H.) in the long sermon of *Ghadīrīya* left explanations and warnings about leadership of Imam 'Alī (P.B.U.H.). But regretfully this Divine leadership–the Greater Hajj–was forgotten in a very short while, and did not last even a day after the demise of the holy Prophet (P.B.U.H. & H.H.)!

Now after more than 1400 years of that bitter landmark, there are still lovers and devotees living on earth who truly try to treat these majesties (P.B.U.T.) in a right manner and perform Hajj in its correct way. On the one hand, when they go to Mecca to perform Hajj, they recognize that Hajj is to renew the promise with the holy Prophet (P.B.U.H. & H.H.) and that Circumambulating around *Ka'ba* [*Ṭawāf*] signifies revolving around, conforming to, and obeying *Ahl al-Bayt* (P.B.U.T.) in all parts of life; on the other hand, when remembering *Ahl al-Bayt* (P.B.U.T.), they know that their confrontation to them (P.B.U.T.) will be like Hajj instructions; moreover when attending their holy shrines they try to pay visit modestly and, in every visit, renew their promise that: my lord, if I was not an obedient servant up to now, and if my sins and transgressions have made me far from you, I would renew my promise to be your real Hajji and spend my whole life for you and stay loyal to you all my life.

7. The Pilgrim as a Soldier

Another valuable attitude toward *Ahl al-Bayt* (P.B.U.T.) is the perspective of being a soldier for them, a soldier always useful and ready for service.

A soldier's major concern is to serve and defend as best as he can, obey his superior and become balanced with him, meaning to forerun his superior as a soldier and to follow him as a follower. One of the features of a prepared soldier is to deliver his paean in the battlefield and when a firm soldier starts to deliver his paean, his friends get encouraged and his enemies disconsolate.

Another good feature of a soldier is that he never says, "I am worried," but he says, "What is our task? We are ready to fight."

A Shiite should always be his Imam's soldier; obeying his Imam, following him as a follower and forerunning and sacrificing his life for his Imam as a soldier. Ma'mūn Raqqī–who is a friend of Imam al-Ṣādiq (P.B.U.H.)–narrates, "One day that I was in the Imam's house a man by the name of Sahl b. Ḥasan al-Khorāsānī came in and complained, "O' Imam, you are too kind and sympathetic, you are of *Ahl al-Bayt* (P.B.U.T.) and you deserve to be the caliph. What has stopped you from uprising and recapturing your right from those imposters and violators while you have more than 100 thousand soldiers in service?" Imam al-Ṣādiq (P.B.U.H.) replied, "Calm down, God keeps your right", and then told one of his servants to ignite the oven; when the fire was flaming, the Imam (P.B.U.H.) ordered Sahl to go and sit in the oven. Sahl said, "O' my lord, don't torture me in fire and forgive me so that God blesses you." In the mean time, another man named Hārūn al-Makkī–barefoot and holding his shoes[1]–came in. The Imam (P.B.U.H.) greeted him and then told him, "Hārūn! Leave your shoes on the ground and move into the oven and stay there." Hārūn left his shoes on the ground and went into the oven and sat there without asking any question. Then the Imam (P.B.U.H.) started speaking about Khorasan as though he had been in Khorasan for a long time and had just come back! After an hour, the Imam (P.B.U.H.) said, "Sahl! Go to the oven and see for yourself." When Sahl looked into the oven, he saw Hārūn sitting in the fire, then the Imam (P.B.U.H.) pointed to Hārūn and said, "Come out and he came out." Then the Imam (P.B.U.H.) turned to Sahl and asked, "How many people do you know in Khorasn as obedient as Hārūn?" Sahl answered, "I swear to God, none! There is not even one man like Hārūn." Then the Imam (P.B.U.H.) said, "Sahl! We know when to rise and that's when we have only *five* obedient and sincere attendants, meanwhile we were and are the most aware of the time."[2]

---

1. Maybe as a sign of respect in the presence of the Imam (P.B.U.H.), as the holy Qur'an says, "So take off your sandals. You are indeed in the sacred valley of Tuwa." (20: 12)
2. *Biḥār al-Anwār*, vol. 47, p. 123.

Yes! An effective soldier should be as such, otherwise like Sahl Ibn Ḥasan, he just makes claim and won't be able to deal with hardships and will leave the scene.

If we look from the viewpoint of a soldier who is serving *Ahl al-Bayt* (P.B.U.T.), we will see that this view is a practical attitude and when the soldier-like pilgrim comes near his chief, he would say, "O' my chief! Just say what I should do." He says, "I haven't come here to merely make a physical and superficial visit to a place! I have much more difficult duties when I see that the hostility of visible and invisible enemies is making trouble." A Shiite soldier should be in the battlefield of Karbala of his own time and should struggle while maintaining Ḥussaini spirit and a sense of rapture.

On the other hand, a soldier should practically prove his power to his chief and verify the fact that he is a faithful and devoted soldier, because when a chief wants to do a difficult work, at first he looks at the soldiers to find the strongest and the readiest, he looks for a soldier whose appearance verifies his ability and readiness and then says, "You! Come here, I want you to do this work." He looks at the soldier's passion to fight and then he plans out the munitions the soldier needs and gives them to him.

The other thing which can be found within the nature of a committed soldier is his ability to make promise and to renew his vow to the chief and his desired ideals. One who goes to the presence of the infallible Imams (P.B.U.T.) and the world protectors using the attitude of a committed soldier, in addition to remembering the ʿAhd Alast or the early pledge he made in the world of *Dharr*, he again renews his pledge[1] and again and again he manfully makes a promise to be a faithful soldier to his protectors and do his best in the way of loyalty and soldiership so that–eventually–all his efforts and devotion will result in the advent of Imam al-Mahdī's (May God hasten his advent) and the establishment of his universal right government.

9. The Pilgrim as a Shiite

Shiism is another attitude which is among the most important perspectives and is regarded to be more comprehensive and inclusive in comparison with the other viewpoints. In other words, we can say all of the mentioned

---

1. Imam Ṣādiq (P.B.U.H.), "Certainly God, the Almighty, has taken a pledge from our followers about Himself and our guardianship as He took the pledge from children of Adam and says in the holy Qurʾan, "When your Lord took from the Children of Adam, from their loins, their descendants and made them bear witness over themselves, [He said to them,] ʿAm I not your Lord?' They said, ʿYes indeed! We bear witness.' [This,] lest you should say on the Day of Resurrection, ʿIndeed we were unaware of this,'" (7: 172) Yes one who honors his pledge about us, God will compensate for what he did with Heaven and fulfill his pledge and one who arouses our anger and feels hostility towards us and doesn't give us our right, he will eternally be punished in the fire of Hell for ever. (*Biḥār al-Anwār*, vol. 2, p. 190)

viewpoints are a branch of the pure tree of this viewpoint.

Human relations have different types in this world. Some of them are arbitrary and manmade and some others are among the real, natural, and divine relations. For example the relation between mankind and the Creator is among the most original and consistent relations which roots in the depth of entity and nature of the human.

According to the Shiite's culture, the relation between the infallible Imams (P.B.U.T.) and the Shiites is an eternal and divine relation. We read in a tradition from Imam al-Ṣādiq (P.B.U.H.) who says,

Our Shiites have been created from the surplus of our clay. Whatever upsets us makes them upset, and whatever pleases us makes them pleased.[1]

This relation is so strong and firm that an Imam can even feel the physical pains of the Shiites. It is quoted from Rumaylah–one of the Shiites of Imam ʿAlī (P.B.U.H.) –saying, "I came down with a high fever. When the fever became mild, I performed *Qusl* (major ablution) and went to the mosque in order to benefit from the reward of Friday Prayer and have the honor of performing my prayer along with my protector, Imam ʿAlī (P.B.U.H.). When he sat on the rostrum and started speaking, my fever became high again. After the prayer, I went to see Imam ʿAlī

---

1. *Al-Amālī*, vol.1, p. 299.

(P.B.U.H.). He asked me about my fever and sickness and I
explained it for him. Then he said, "O' Rumaylah! When
every believer becomes sick, accordingly, we get sick and
their sorrow and grief makes us sad and unhappy, and we
say Amen after every supplication that they make and if
they don't supplicate, we pray for them."[1]

This holy and deep relation regards the souls of the
Imams (P.B.U.T.) and their Shiites as a single soul and connects them so firmly that Abū Baṣīr–who was one of the
companions of Imam al-Ṣādiq (P.B.U.H.)–says, "In a meet-
ing, I asked him (P.B.U.H.), "How is it that we sometimes
suddenly feel sad and unhappy or unexpectedly become
happy and glad without any certain reason?" His emi-
nence answered: "This sadness and gladness that sometimes comes to you is the result of the sadness and gladness which comes to us, and that's due to the fact that
both we and you are created from the light of God, the
Almighty, and He has made our clay and your clay one"[2].

So it can be said that when we are thinking about *Ahl
al-Bayt* (P.B.U.T.) and their greatness and magnanimity, or

---

1. *Irshād al-Qulūb*, vol. 2, p. 282.
2. *Biḥār al-Anwār*, vol. 58, p. 145; in another tradition, Imam Ṣādiq (P.B.U.H.) said,
"Indeed Almighty God created us from the clay of '*Illīyūn* and created our souls
from clay that is superior to that and also created the souls of our Shiites from
the clay of '*Iilliyūn* and created their body from inferior clay than that. Therefore there is a close relationship between us and our Shiites and their hearts
are desirous of us." (*Al-Kāfī*, volume 1, p. 389.)

remembering their tragedies and griefs and our heart is attentively beating for them, it's due to the mentioned severe spiritual connection between us and them. In fact, it shows their graces and kindness toward us. Of course we are supposed to provide the prerequisites for these graces and favors, and by preparing the land of our heart, we have to develop a suitable condition so that the seed of their affection can grow in it and, accordingly, we can practically follow them.

The most interesting point is that not only Imam al-Mahdī (May God hasten his advent) thinks about us when we are thinking about his holy essence but also he thinks about us when we are ignorant of him. Even in that time, he thinks about us and does what is advisable and good for us as he stated through a letter to al-Shaykh al-Mufīd, "We will not neglect your affairs and never forget you."[1]

With this introduction, the first question that may be posed is this, "What do we mean by Shiite and how should a Shiite behave in the presence of *Ahl al-Bayt* (P.B.U.T.)?"

---

1. *Al-Iḥtijāj*, vol. 2, p. 497.

The Conception of Shiite in Verses and Traditions

In the Arabic language, "the shiite" of someone literally means, "the follower" of that person[1]. In a tradition, the holy Prophet (P.B.U.H. & H.H.) has said,

إِنَّ شِيعَتَنَا مَنْ شَيَّعَنَا وَتَبِعَنَا فِي أَعْمَالِنَا

Certainly our Shiites are those who follow us and adhere to us in our acts.[2]

In the holy Qur'an we have two words which are close to "shiite" in meaning and they are "اطاعت" (*iṭāʿat*, meaning obedience) and "تبعيّت" (*tabaʿīyyat*, meaning adherence). From what has been mentioned about these two words within the lexicons and based on their usage in the holy Qur'an, we can get the precise meaning of each:

The precise Meaning of Obedience

Obedience means listening and obeying. In some of the verses of the holy Quran we can see this meaning,

وَقَالُوا سَمِعْنَا وَأَطَعْنَا

And they say" ,We hear and obey (2 :285) ".

1. Ibn Manẓūr, M., (1996), *Lisān al-ʿArab*, Beirut: Dār Iḥyāʾ al-Turāth al-ʿArabī, vol.7, p. 258.
2. Imam al-Ḥasan al-ʿAskarī, (1409 A.H.) *Tafsīr al-Imām al-Ḥasan al-ʿAskarī*, Qom: Madrasa al-Imām al-Mahdī, vol. 1, p. 307.

The Arabs, also, use such a meaning in their colloquial speech, for instance when an Arab wants to value and follow the words of another person or exaggerate in compliment, he says, "سمعاً وطاعتا" which means "I listen and do (what has been said)" and if we want to say it in a colloquial way, it means "okay, as you wish; you order and we carry it out", which means to be an absolutely submissive slave. In comparison to *adherence*, *obedience* implies less thinking and the obedient person should unconditionally follow what the protector orders.

As we discussed before, the product of obedience is the companionship with *Ahl al-Bayt* (P.B.U.T.):

And whoever *obeys* Allah and the Apostle, these are with those upon whom Allah has bestowed favors from among the prophets and the truthful and the martyrs and the good, and a goodly company are they! (4: 69)

The Precise Meaning of Adherence

Some words have both negative and positive forms, and the word of *adherence* is so. In verse 21 of *Sūra Nūr*, our Almighty God says about the negative form of adherence:

يا أَيُّها الَّذِينَ آمَنُوا لاتَتَّبِعُوا خُطُواتِ الشَّيطانِ وَ مَن يَتَّبِع خُطُواتِ الشَّيطانِ فَإِنَّهُ يَأْمُرُ بِالفَحشاءِ وَ المُنكَرِ...

O' you who believe! Do not follow the footsteps of the Shaitan, and

whoever follows the footsteps of the Shaitan, then surely he bids the doing of indecency and evil....

Let's think more about the concept of footstep. Is it a matter of 'listening and doing' or 'looking and doing'? Definitely 'looking and doing'! Hence here we have the conception of "looking and doing" and *adherence* means "look and do".

If one wants to walk behind another person and tries not to leave any trace of them, what would they do? Apparently they would follow in the footsteps of that person who is walking ahead of them. Thus from the aspect of product, *adherence* is stronger than *obedience*; as we said, the product of the latter is "companionship" whereas the product of the former is "unity" or to become exactly similar to a person who has been followed, not to be only along with them but to become exactly like them or having the same quality as they have.

In the case posed in this verse, the product is to become the same as Satan or turning into indecency and evil acts.

This matter, in its positive aspect, can be verified through verse 36 of *Ṣūra Ibrāhīm* where Prophet Abraham (P.B.U.H.) says,

فَمَن تَبِعَنِي فَإِنَّهُ مِنِّي وَمَنْ عَصَانِي فَإِنَّكَ غَفُورٌ رَّحِيمٌ

So whoever follows me indeed belongs to me, and as for those who disobey me, well, You are indeed All-forgiving, All-merciful.

And this is the secret of Salmān al-Fārsī's spiritual growth who followed the matter of *adherence* and arrived at a position that the holy Prophet (B.P.U.H. & H.H.) says about him,

سَلمانُ مِنّا اهلَ البَيت

Salmān is from us, the *Ahl al-Bayt.* (P.B.U.T.) [1]

The Precise Meaning of Shiite

The same concept has been mentioned into several verses and traditions to explain the meaning of Shia and the positive adherence. For instance, we just read a tradition from the holy Prophet (P.B.U.H. & H.H.) in which he says, "Certainly our Shiites are those who follow us and adhere to us in our deeds."[2] Why is Salmān said to be one of *Ahl al-Bayt* (P.B.U.T.)? Because he followed the holy Prophet and Imam ʿAlī (P.B.U.T.) and put his feet wherever they put their feet. It has been narrated from Salmān that "Once I was with Imam ʿAlī (P.B.U.H.) that he was suddenly summoned by the holy Prophet (P.B.U.H. & H.H.) to do an

---

1. *Kashf al-Qummah*, vol. 1, pp. 96, 389.
2. *Tafsīr al-Imām al-Ḥasan al-ʿAskarī (P.B.U.H.)*, vol.1, p. 307.

important task. When the Imam (P.B.U.H.) decided to leave, he asked me to follow him and put my feet exacly where he put his feet so that no traces of my feet would be left! And I did so.[1]" This way of following, apart from its actual meaning, may bear a metaphorical sense.

It means that you must only follow *Ahl al-Bayt* (P.B.U.T.), set all your affairs in accordance with them, always try to become exactly similar to these holy dignitaries in all aspects of your life, and also attempt not to leave even a trace from yourself in the monotheistic system of God. This is 'adherence' and Salmān (P.B.U.H.) is a true follower and a true Shiite. That's why Imam ʿAlī (P.B.U.H.) says about him,

> Salmān is taught the first and the last knowledge, he is a sea whose
> end is imperceptible ... Salmān is from us, *Ahl al-Bayt* (P.B.U.T.).[2]

Shiites Need to Follow *Ahl Al-Bayt* (P.B.U.T.) in Every Aspect of Their Life

As it is inferred from the previously-mentioned traditions, the Shiites are a part of the entity of *Ahl al-Bayt* (P.B.U.T.). In another tradition, we read,

> They have been named Shia, because they are created out of our
> light beam.[3]

1. Baḥrānī, H. (1413 A.H.), *Madīnata Maʿājiz al-'A'immat al-'Ithnā ʿAshar*, Qom: Muassisa al-Maʿārif al-Islāmīya, vol. 2, pp. 9-10.
2. *Biḥār al-Anwār*, vol. 22, p. 348.
3. Ḥāfiẓ Bursī, R., (1422 A.H.), *Mashāriq Anwār al-Yaqīn fī Asrār Amīr al-Muʾminīn*

Humans have numerous aspects and dimentions, from their physical body to their spiritual, emotional, and moral dimentions. According to this tradition, in addition, Shiites have some other dimensions including the "light dimension".

To nourish and improve the "light dimention", Shiites must derive benefits from the light of *Ahl al-Bayt* (P.B.U.T.) and get close to them, a fact clearly found in the adventure of Imam al-Ḥussain (P.B.U.H.). In the short period of moving toward Karbala, the companions of Imam al-Ḥussain (P.B.U.H.) became so pure and sacred through being nourished from the light of Imam al-Ḥussain (P.B.U.H.) that it led them to become similar to their protector. Imam al-Ḥussain (P.B.U.H.) answered to Muḥammad b. Ḥanafīyah about them,

> They are my Shiites whose order and decision are my order and
> decision.[1]

Therefore, the light of Imam is the origin of Shiites and their photic dimension needs to be more nourished in comparison with the lower dimensions and this nourishment happens through the light of *Imamate*. So they have to get everything from one source, only *Ahl al-Bayt* (P.B.U.T.). That is why Imam ʿAlī (P.B.U.H.) says to Kumayl,

---

(P.B.U.H.), Beirut: Aʿlamī, , p. 65.
1. *Biḥār al-Anwār*, vol. 44, p. 324.

O' Kumayl! Don't get anything from anyone else but us so that you
can become one of us![1]

What does it mean? Does it mean that only follow our traditions and study them and no more? No! It isn't the purpose! It means that not only don't get the recognition, edification and guidance from other than us, but also take no notice of something such as in 'my' opinion, 'my' thoughts, 'my' morality, 'my' preference and 'my' spirit and even 'my' intention and get all of them from us, it means that even get your personality from us; otherwise, anything that is got from anyone else except *Ahl al-Bayt* (P.B.U.T.) is called referring to *Ṭaghūt* and doesn't have any reliability.

God, the Almighty, says in the verse 256 of *Sūra* Baqarah (second verse of *Āyat Al-Kursī*):

There is no compulsion in religion, rectitude has become distinct from error. So one who disavows fake deities (*Ṭaghūt*) and has faith in Allah has held fast to the firmest handle for which there is no breaking; and Allah is All-hearing, All-knowing.

According to traditions, 'the firmest handle for which there is no breaking' is *Ahl al-Bayt* (P.B.U.T.). [2]

But why does the Chief of the Faithful (P.B.U.H.) say that Shiites shouldn't get anything other than *Ahl al-Bayt*

---

1. *Tuḥaf al-ʿUqūl*, p. 171.
2. *Al-Kāfī*, volume 8, p. 124.

(P.B.U.T.)? To answer this question, it should be said because Shiites are the light beam of their Imam and–as we know–a light should only be nourished from its source because it has emitted from the source of light and it will return to it.[1]

The existential dimensions of a real Shiite, including their words, deeds, attributes, possessions and demands should evidently portray an Imam's self, words, deeds, attributes, possessions and demands. As a person sees the light beam of the sun through a window in the morning, the first thing that draws his attention to itself is the sun! Therefore, at the time of watching this scene, that person won't say that the particles of photons are coming or the light beam is coming but he will say, "The sun has risen." He will conclude the source of light from its beams. A Shiite is like this. He is the light beam of his Imam, he is a channel for those beams, he is a part of the body of the Imam and if he unconditionally submits to the Imam, the light of the Imam will radiate from his window and will take care of everything.

If one really wants to be a Shiite, his behaviors, desires, moralities, intentions and all his demands and posses-

1. Imam Ṣādiq (P.B.U.H.) has said, "O' Mufadhal! We have been created from the light of God and our Shiites have been created from a lower light of our light. O' Mufadhal! Our Shiites are from us and we are from our Shiites, haven't you ever seen the place where the sun rises?" Mufadhal answered, "The sun rises in the east." Imam (P.B.U.H.) said, "And where does it return?" Mafzal says: "in the west."[and again tomorrow rises from the east] Imam (P.B.U.H.) said, "Our Shiites are just like the sun, they rise from us and also they will return to us." *Biḥār al-Anwār*, vol. 25, p. 21.

sions should be close to the Imam or–to say the matter more accurately–his whole entity should exactly be the manifestation of the Imam's entity. There must be a unity in essence. We must be as such, as the Chief of the Faithful (P.B.U.H.) said,

The friends are, in fact, the same, even though they have been put into different bodies.[1]

Therefore, according to the attitude of *Shiite*, there is no concept of multiple personalities, rather, there is the concept of multiple bodies. It means that there shouldn't be anything like "I" and "you" but the Imam should only be important and although many people seemingly move around him, yet if we look at these people from the perspective of being Shiites, we see the sun and its light beams.

While approaching the Imam, a Shiite should consider himself as a small river connected to a vast ocean. He should wholeheartedly believe that such river should be well-nourished from that vast ocean. Both the river and the ocean contain water but their capacities differ. In the same way that the river connects to the ocean to become filled with water, the river of our heart would also be filled with sprituallity should it get connected to the Imams through pilgrimage.

---

1. Āmidī, A., (1410 A.H.), *Ghurar al-Ḥikam wa Durar al-Kalim*, Qom: Dār al-Kitāb al-Islāmī, p. 115.

According to the words of *Ahl al-Bayt* (P.B.U.T.), when we return to them, stand in their presence in their holy shrine, and hug their lovely *Dharīh*, they would check our deeds and see if our entity is the same as theirs. They would see if our hearts have been nurchured merely through *Ahl al-Bayt* (P.B.U.T.) or not. We read in *al-Jāmi ʿa al-Kabīrah* statement of tribute (a comprehensive statement of tribute narrated from Imam al-Hādī (P.B.U.H.) addressing all the Infallibles (P.B.U.T.) and is advised to be recited in all shrines of them),

إيابُ الخَلقِ اَلَيكُم وَحِسابُهُم عَلَيكُم

The ultimate destination of the creatures is to you, and calling them to account is your mission.[1]

Eventually, all of the creatures will return to *Ahl al-Bayt* (P.B.U.T.) in the Hereafter, and on that occasion, they will check them out. We wish that we will have lived and behaved in a way that the holy progeny of the Prophet (P.B.U.T.) regard us as Salmān (P.B.U.H.) and say that, "You are from us, *Ahl al-Bayt* (P.B.U.T.)."

---

1. *Tahdhīb al-Ahkām,* vol.6, p. 95.

The Effects and Rewards of Visiting the Holy Shrines of *Ahl al-Bayt* (P.B.U.T.)

In the final steps of our journey to "*high above the heavens*", it's time to breathe in the fragrant garden of traditions describing the blessings a pilgrim receives on his visit to the holy shrines of *Ahl al-Bayt* (P.B.U.T.) so that when we descend and come back on earth we have enough energy and motivation to soon again restart this long but 'beneficial' journey. Of course these are only a drop of the ocean of rewards and blessings. Also even all that have been mentioned is what could be somehow digested by our limited minds, otherwise, the real gifts for *Zīyārah* are much beyond our understanding.

1. Visiting the Holy Prophet (P.B.U.H. & H.H.)

A) Imam al-Ṣādiq (P.B.U.H.) said, "Imam al-Ḥussain (P.B.U.H.) asked the holy Prophet (P.B.U.H. & H.H.), 'O my father! What is the reward of the one who visits you?' The holy Prophet (P.B.U.H. & H.H.) replied, 'O my son! One who pays me a visit while I am alive or dead, it's my duty to visit them in the Hereafter and give them a release from their troubles and difficulties.'[1]

B) It has been narrated from Zayd b. Hishām who said,

---

[1] *Kāmil al-Zīyārāt*, p. 14.

"I asked Imam al-Ḥussain (P.B.U.H.) what the reward of the one who comes to visit the holy shrine of the Prophet (P.B.U.H. & H.H.) is. Imam (P.B.U.H.) answered, 'The visitor of the holy Prophet (P.B.U.H. & H.H.) is the same as thec one who has visited God, the Almighty, on top of the Divine Throne.'"[1]

2. Visiting the Chief of the Faithful (P.B.U.H.)

Yūnus b. Abū Wahb al-Qaṣrī says, "Once I entered the city of Medina and went to see Imam al-Ṣādiq (P.B.U.H.) and said to him, "May I be sacrificed for you, I have come to visit you but I didn't go to visit the Chief of the Faithful (P.B.U.H.)." The Imam (P.B.U.H.) said, "You have made a big mistake, if you weren't from our Shiites, I wouldn't even look at you; why don't you visit the dignitary whom God and His angels and messengers and believers visit?" I replied, "May I be sacrificed for you, I wasn't aware of this matter." He said, "You have to know that–in the view of God–the Chief of the Faithful (P.B.U.H.) is superior to all Imams (P.B.U.T.)."[2]

---

1. Ibid., p. 15.
2. *Al-Kāfī*, vol. 4, p. 579.

3. Visiting the Imams[1] (P.B.U.H.) Buried in *Baqī'* Cemetery

Imam al-Ṣādiq (P.B.U.H.) has said, "Whenever you go to visit the tombs of the Imams (P.B.U.T.) buried in Baqī' Cemetery, stand and place the Qibla to your back and turn to the tombs and then say, "Peace be upon you, O', Imams of guidance! Peace be upon you, O', people of piety! Peace be upon you, O', proofs of Allah on the people of the earth! Peace be upon you, O', the family of the Prophet of Allah! I bear witness that you proclaimed and advised and persevered for the sake of Allah, and that you were belied and evil was done to you, and you forgave; and I bear witness that you are the rightly guided leaders, and that obedience to you is incumbent, and that your speech is correct, and that you invited (to the truth) but were not answered, and you commanded but were not followed. I bear witness that you are the pillars of religion and support of the earth, you were always under the (caring) eyes of Allah. You have become pure; your origin is pure. Through you He has favored us. He has created you 'in houses Allah has allowed to be raised and wherein His Name is celebrated.' (24:36). He has made our salutations to you to be mercy for us and expiation of our sins, for Allah has chosen you for us, and has made our creation pure because He has

---

1. Imam Ḥasan al-Mujtabā, Imam 'Alī b. al-Ḥusain, Imam Bāqir, and Imam Ṣādiq (P.B.U.T.).

favored us with your affection. We are named in front of Him due to your gnosis and because we acknowledged and believed in you..."[1]

4. Visiting Imam al-Ḥussain (P.B.U.H.)

A) It is narrated from Imam al-Ṣādiq (P.B.U.H.) that he said, "One who wants to be in the vicinity of the holy Prophet (P.B.U.H. & H.H.) and Imam ʻAlī (P.B.U.H.) and Lady Fāṭima (P.B.U.H.), they shouldn't abandon visiting Imam al-Ḥussain(P.B.U.H.)."[2]

B) Imam al-Kāẓim (P.B.U.H.) has stated, "One who visits Imam al-Ḥussain (P.B.U.H.) and is aware of his right, Allah will forgive their past and future[3] sins."[4]

5. Visiting Imam al-Kāẓim (P.B.U.H.)

Ḥasan b. ʻAlī al-Washshā' has narrated, "In the presence of Imam al-Riḍā (P.B.U.H.), I asked him what the reward of the one who visits the tomb of your father Imam al-Kāẓim (P.B.U.H.) is. The Imam (P.B.U.H.) answered, "Visit him... the reward and superiority of one who visits him is equal to the reward of one who visits the tomb of Imam al-Ḥussain (P.B.U.H.)."[5]

---

1. *Kāmil al-Zīyārāt*, vol. 1, p. 53.
2. Ibid., p. 136.
3. Of course, it is not a permission to commit more sins in the future. Indeed, it means that Allah would guarantee to forgive those future sins of the Imam's (P.B.U.H.) pilgrims which are the result of negligence.
4. Ibid., p. 138.
5. Ibid., p. 299.

6. Visiting Imam 'Alī b. Mūsā al-Riḍā (P.B.U.H.)

"Imam al-Riḍā (P.B.U.H.) has stated, "One who visits me while my home is distant and my tomb is far away, I will visit him in three times of the Doomsday to preserve him from its dreads and fears:

1. When the record of actions is delivered to the right and left hands,

2. When passing *al-Ṣirāṭ* (a bridge over the Hell that all people should cross on the Day of Resurrection; some people cross fast, some will stay there for thousands of years, and some will fall from the bridge to the Hell.)

3. When measuring deeds.[1]

7. Visiting Imam Muḥammad b. 'Alī al-Jawād (P.B.U.H.)

Ibrāhīm b. 'Uqbah says, "I wrote a letter to Imam al-Hādī (P.B.U.H.) and asked him about visiting the holy shrine of Imam al-Ḥussain (P.B.U.H.) and visiting the holy shrine of Kazimayn. He answered: "Visiting Imam al-Ḥussain (P.B.U.H.) has priority, but it [Kāẓimayn] includes the visit of two dignitaries, [Imam al-Kāẓim and Imam al-Jawād (P.B.U.T.)], and has a bigger reward.[2]

---

1. Ibid.
2. Majlisī, M. T. (1414 A.H.), *Lawame Sahebqarany*, Qom: Ismaeilian, vol. 8, p. 567. See also, *Al-Kāfī*, vol. 4, p. 583.

8. Visiting Imam al-Hādī (P.B.U.H.)

Imam al-Hādī (P.B.U.H.) is reported to have said, "I have besought Allah, the Almighty and All-majestic, not to disappoint any one who says this prayer in my shrine,

O', my means when I lack means! O', my hope and my trust! O', my haven and my support! O' One! O', One and Only! O', Qul huwa Allahu aḥad [Say, 'He is Allah, the One.'] (112: 1) I beseech You in the name of those whom You created from among Your creations, but You have not made anyone to be like them at all, (please do) send blessings upon them all... [Now you may submit your requests before Almighty Allah])"[1]

9. Visiting Imam Ḥasan al-'Askarī (P.B.U.H.)

Imam Ḥasan al-'Askarī (P.B.U.H.) has stated, "My tomb is in *Surra Man Ra'ā* [the city of Samarra] which is the cause of protection for both sides."[2] [Both Shiites and Sunnies[3]]

There are plenty of other traditions regarding the reward of visiting the holy shrines of *Ahl al-Bayt* (P.B.U.T.); you may refer to the traditional books.

---

1. *Al-Amālī* (Ṭūsī), vol. 1, p. 285.
2. *Tahdhīb Al-Aḥkām*, vol. 6, p. 93.
3. *Lawame Sahebqarany*, vol. 8, p. 567.

HIGH ABOVE THE HEAVENS

List of Resources

Arabic References

1. *The holy Qur'an*, trans., Ali Quli Qarai, (2013), Mashhad: Behnashr.

2. Āmidī, 'Abd al-Wahid., (1410 A.H.), *Ghurar al-Ḥikam wa Durar al-Kalim*, Qom: Dār al-Kitāb al-Islāmī.

3. 'Ayyāshī, Muḥammad. (1380 A.H.), *Tafsīr Al-'Ayyashī*, Tehran: al-Matba'a al-'Ilmīyya.

4. Baḥrānī, Hāshim. (1374 A.H. (solar)), *Al-Burhān fī Tafsīr al-Qur'an*, Qom: Be'that.

5. Baḥrānī, Hāshim. (1413 A.H.), *Madīnata Ma'ājiz al-A'immat al-'Ithnā 'Ashar*, Qom: Muassisa al-Ma'ārif al-Islāmīya.

6. Daylamī, Ḥasan. (1412 A.H.), *Irshād al-Qulūb*, Qom: al-Sharīf al-Raḍī.

7. Ḥāfiẓ Bursī, Rajab. (1422 A.H.), *Mashāriq Anwār al-Yaqīn fī Asrār Amīr al-Mu'minīn*(P.B.U.H.).

8. Ibn Abī Jumhūr al-Aḥsā'ī, Muḥammad. (1405 A.H.), *'Awālī al-La'ālī al-'azīzīyya fī al-Aḥādīth al-dīnīyya*, Qom: Dār Sayyid al-Shuhadā.

9. Ibn Ḥamza Ṭūsī, Muḥammad. (1419 A.H.), *Al-Thāqib fī al-Manāqib*, Qom: Ansariyan.

10. Ibn Manẓūr, Muḥammad. (1996), *Lisān al-'Arab*, Beirut: Dār Iḥyā' al-Turāth al-'Arabī.

11. Ibn Qūlawayh, Ja'far. (1356 A.H. (solar)), *Kāmil al-Zīyārāt*, Najaf: Dār al-Murtaḍavīyya.

12. Ibn Shahrāshūb, Muḥammad. (1379 A.H.), *Manāqib Āle Abī Ṭālib*, Qom: 'Allāma.

13. Ibn Shu'be, Ḥasan. (1404 A.H.), *Tuḥaf al-'Uqūl*, Qom: Jāmi'i Mudarrisīn.

14. Ibn Ṭāwūs, 'Alī. (1373 A.H. (solar)), *Iqbāl al-A'māl*, Tehran: Būstān Kitāb.

15. Imam al-Ḥasan al-'Askarī, (1409 A.H.) *Tafsīr al-Imām al-Ḥasan al-'Askarī*, Qom: Madrasa al-Imām al-Mahdī.

16. Irbilī, 'Alī. (1381 A.H.), *Kashf al-Qummah*, Tabriz: Banīhāshimī.

17. Kaf'amī, Ibrāhīm. (1405 A.H.), *al-Miṣbāḥ*, Qom: Dār Al-Raḍī.

18. Khaṣībī, Ḥussain. (1377 A.H. (solar)), *Al-Hidāyat Al-Kubrā*, Beirut: Al-Balāq.

19. Kūfī, Furāt., (1410 A.H.), *Tafsīr Furāt al-Kūfī*, Tehran: Ministry of Islamic Guidance Pub.

20. Kulaynī, Muḥammad. (1407 A.H.), *Al-Kāfī*, Tehran: Dār al-Kutub al-Islāmīya.

21. Majlisī, Muḥammad Bāqir. (1403 A.H.), *Biḥār al-Anwār al-Jāmi'ah li-Durar Akhbār al-A'immat al-Aṭhār*, Beirut: Dār Iḥyā' al-Turāth al-'Arabī.

22. Qumī, 'Abbās. (2010 A.H.), *Mafātīḥ al-Jinān* (Badr Shahin trans.), Qom: Ansariyan.

23. Ṣadūq, Muḥammad. (1403 A.H.), *Ma'ānī al-Akhbār*, Qom: Daftar Intishārāt Islāmī.

24. Ṣadūq, Muḥammad. (1406 A.H.), *Thawāb al-A'māl wa-'Iqāb al-A'māl*, Qom: Sharīf Al-Rāḍī.

25. Ṣadūq, Muḥammad. (1413 A.H.), *Man Lā Yaḥduruhū al-Faqīh*, Qom: Daftar Intishārāt Islāmī.

26. Ṣadūq, Muḥammad. (1378 A.H.), *'Uyūn Akhbār al-Riḍā* (P.B.U.H.), Tehran: Jahān.

27. Al-Shahīd al-Awwal, Muḥammad. (1410 A.H.), *Al-Mazār fī kayfiyyati zīyārāt al-Nabī wa al-A'imma*, Qom: Madrasa Imām al-Mahdī.

28. Al-Sharīf al-Raḍī, Muḥammad. (1414 A.H.), *Nahj al-Balāghah* (research by Ṣubḥī Ṣāliḥ), Qom: Hijra.

29. Shaykh Ḥurr al-'Āmilī, Muḥammad. (1425 A.H.), *Ithbāt al-hudāt bi al-Nuṣūṣ wa al-Mu'jizāt*, Beirut: A'lamī.

30. Ṭabarī al-Ṣaghīr, Muḥammad. (1413 A.H.), *Dalā'il al-Imāma*, Qom: Bi'that.

31. Ṭabrisī, Aḥmad. (1403 A.H.), *Al-Iḥtijāj 'Alā Ahl Al-Lijāj*, Mashhad: Al-Murtaḍā pub

32. Ṭūsī, Muḥammad. (1407 A.H.), *Tahdhīb Al-Aḥkām*, Tehran: Dār al-Kutub al-Islāmīya

33. Ṭūsī, Muḥammad. (1414 A.H.), *Al-Amālī*, Qum: Dar Al-Thiqāfa

Persian References

1. Majlisī, Muḥammad Taqī. (1414 A.H.), *Lawame Sahebqarany*, Qom: Ismaeilian.

2. Muhammadi Ishtihardi, Muhammad., (1381 A.H. (solar)), *Dastan Dustan*, Qom: Bustan Ketab